SECOND CHANCES

NEW DIRECTIONS IN THE HUMAN-ANIMAL BOND

A dynamic relationship has always existed between people and animals. Each influences the psychological and physiological state of the other. Published in collaboration with Purdue University's College of Veterinary Medicine, New Directions in the Human-Animal Bond expands our knowledge of the interrelationships between people, animals, and their environment. Scholarly works, memoirs, practitioner guides, and books written for a general audience are welcomed on all aspects of human-animal interaction and welfare.

SERIES EDITOR

Alan M. Beck, Purdue University

OTHER TITLES IN THIS SERIES

Animal-Assisted Counseling and Psychotherapy: A Clinician's Guide
Linda Chassman Craddock and Ellen Kinney Winston

A History of the Development of Alternatives to Animals in Research and Testing
John Parascandola

Fine Horses and Fair-Minded Riders: Modern Vaquero Horsemanship
JuliAnna Ávila

My One-Eyed, Three-Legged Therapist: How My Cat Clio Saved Me
Kathy M. Finley

Identity, Gender, and Tracking: The Reality of Boundaries for Veterinary Students
Jenny R. Vermilya

Dogs and Cats in South Korea: Itinerant Commodities
Julien Dugnoille

Assessing Handlers for Competence in Animal-Assisted Interventions
Ann R. Howie

The Canine-Campus Connection: Roles for Dogs in the Lives of College Students
Mary Renck Jalongo (Ed.)

Pioneer Science and the Great Plagues:
How Microbes, War, and Public Health Shaped Animal Health
Norman F. Cheville

SECOND CHANCES

The Transformative Relationship Between Incarcerated Youth and Shelter Dogs

Joan K. Dalton

Purdue University Press • West Lafayette, Indiana

Printed in the United States of America.

Cataloging-in-Publication Data is available from the Library of Congress.
978-1-62671-105-1 (paperback)
978-1-62671-106-8 (epub)
978-1-62671-107-5 (epdf)

Cover: Tim saying goodbye to his dog Cleo. (Photo from author's collection.)

To Oregon Youth Authority administrators Rick Hill, Robert Jester, Gary Lawhead, and Lord High School Principal John Pendergrass for their openness to considering dogs as a means of rehabilitation for male juvenile offenders at MacLaren Youth Correctional Facility. And to the youth who opened their hearts and minds to saving dogs while also saving themselves and moving on to a promising life outside corrections.

Contents

Project POOCH Timeline

1993 The Project POOCH (standing for "Positive Opportunities—Obvious Change with Hounds") program began with one dog and one student. The program was funded by the high school budget administered by John Pendergrass (principal) and Joan Dalton (vice principal). The program became an alternative way for selected students to earn high school credit by working with dogs for half days and working at the high school, completing traditional academic studies for the other half of school days. Those in Project POOCH earned credit in communications, careers, and work experience. Later, they earned a quarter credit in science for the DNA study of dogs. The school budget funded a full-time special education teacher and dog expert Monday through Friday. Weekends, holidays, and sick days were covered by a teaching assistant (TA).

1994 Measure 11: Oregon's mandatory minimum sentencing law established sentences for twenty-four felonies. It requires that any youth fifteen years or older, charged with a Measure 11 crime, be automatically prosecuted as an adult.

1995 The school continued to fund the daily staffing and weekends with teaching assistants. However, none of the staff had dog training experience or the willingness to take paid dog training classes. Teaching assistants were hired as temps without benefits and allowed to work for six months. After the six months were up, another one was hired. An employee of the Willamette Humane Society agreed to volunteer once a week to provide consistent dog training since the original teacher for the program became a full-time writer of individual education plans (IEPs) for students.

1997 Joan Dalton was moved from vice principalship at the high school located on the MacLaren campus to an office in Salem to plan the education departments of five new regional juvenile corrections facilities located throughout Oregon. Due to too many instances of weekend staff absenteeism, Joan supervised students and dogs in Project POOCH on weekends. Money for staff was also an issue from time to time.

1998 After completing the planning and implementation of the five new education departments in the regional facilities, Joan Dalton received a layoff notice in July from the Oregon Department of Education, now overseeing the high school at MacLaren. On October 26, 1998, Project POOCH was incorporated as a 501 (C) (3) nonprofit organization. Joan remained active at the kennel as she built a board of directors for the newly formed nonprofit organization.

1999 The teaching assistant working Monday through Friday had temp status with no benefits and resigned. All dogs were adopted in July, and no new ones were accepted due to the lack of staff. Joan Dalton continued efforts to get the Oregon Youth Authority to include staffing for Project POOCH in their budget. In October, John Pendergrass (now working in Salem for the Oregon Department of Education) agreed to provide a full-time teaching assistant position outside his budget. The Oregon Youth Authority continued to provide security and space for the kennel.

2000 Joan Dalton became executive director and established an office off campus.

2020 A new executive director was hired. Joan continued mentoring released youths.

Author's Note

Dear Reader,

Please note that I have faithfully transcribed notes, letters, and interviews as presented to me from those I have written about in this book. The names of juvenile offenders (except for two) have been changed to protect their identities.

Joan

1

My Path to Corrections

Winter 1990

GANGS IN PORTLAND

In the late 1980s, the gangs (Kerby Blocc Crips and the Richmonds) surfaced in Portland, Oregon. Handguns, drugs, auto theft, and reckless endangerment became a common occurrence. Some of the young people were sentenced to MacLaren School for Boys in Woodburn, Oregon—the strictest juvenile incarceration facility in Oregon.

By 1988, gangs had emerged as a major problem, especially in the Portland metropolitan area. Jennifer Bjorhus, an Oregonian newsperson, noted, "The Richmonds were midlevel crack-cocaine dealers who first surfaced in Portland around 1992. Police called them Richmonds because some of their core members came from the Richmond area in California. At the time, they were considered the most feared and dangerous criminal organization in Northeast Portland."

MacLaren School for Boys (later changed to MacLaren Youth Correctional Facility) was where those ordered to do serious time in corrections were to be placed. Many of the incarcerated came from the largest county (Multnomah) in Oregon. According to the Oregon Youth Authority 1995–1997 biennial report, "Governor Barbara Roberts appointed a Task Force on Juvenile Crime in 1993. Chaired by Attorney General Ted Kulongoski, the focus of the Task Force was to expand the capacity of Oregon's juvenile institutions to meet growing needs and to ensure youth offenders are held accountable throughout the juvenile justice system. The Task Force recommended changes to Oregon's juvenile justice system in light of the increase in violent juvenile crime."

I worked on my administrative credentials at Portland State University to become a school administrator. After completing the program, I was ready to move from teaching to joining a high school leadership team. I had heard of a vice principal opening at the high school at a juvenile facility in Woodburn, Oregon. I was invited for an informal interview to tour the high school and campus at the MacLaren School for Boys.

A few days later, I warmed up my Toyota Celica and headed to Woodburn, a small rural town about twenty-five miles south of Portland. The only way to get there from Portland is by automobile. I passed small stores where workers would drop in for fast food, beer, and a lottery ticket. I passed a motel offering a clean room and HBO. The farm stands where fresh produce, plants, and eggs were sold had closed for the winter months. I gasped at a dead cat left alongside the two-lane highway.

I turned in the driveway to the MacLaren School for Boys. I felt my body tense, knowing I was about to enter a place where teenage boys were living due to committing a crime. The campus was unfenced, so I drove up the short driveway and parked my car in the visitor section. As advised ahead of time, I locked my handbag in the trunk of my car.

The school principal, John Pendergrass, met me at the entrance to check me in. I was given a bright yellow visitor badge so people could identify me as a visitor. We walked past the gym to the entrance of the high school. In the distance, I could see eight brick living units, each housing twenty-five boys. The central administration building was painted white. It contained a canteen, a mail room, and offices for administrative staff. I would soon learn about the school's history.

The 1889 legislature appropriated $30,000, and a reform school was established to provide youth with a structured living environment where they could receive an education and develop self-respect, a good work ethic, and a desire for success once they returned to society.

Commitments to the State Reform School quickly overwhelmed its capacity. On October 1, 1892, it was announced that no more boys would be received until the legislature secured additional space. The school was renamed the Oregon State Training School and moved from Salem to Woodburn in the 1920s. The length of stay averaged twelve to twenty-four months, and programs emphasized academic and vocational training.

In 1951, the school became MacLaren School for Boys in honor of Scottish-born Reverend William MacLaren. He had worked many years with troubled youth in Oregon.

LORD HIGH SCHOOL

The high school is a one-level building built into a T shape. It was built much later than the administration building and is named Lord High School. All boys without a high school diploma or GED are required to attend classes. The classes can accommodate as many as fifteen students in a social studies class or as few as five in remedial reading. Many of the students are on individual education plans (IEPs) due to cognitive disabilities.

On the day of my visit, John and I stood at the school entrance as students returned from lunch in their living units. The boys entered the building by living unit. Once the first unit was inside, the next could enter. Very few of the boys appeared happy about coming to school.

The teachers stood by the classroom doors until everyone was where they were assigned. The boys mostly wore gray sweatpants and white T-shirts. Some wore flip-flops. If they wore lavender T-shirts, they were escorted to a nearby two-story wooden building where the sex offenders went to school. These students had to walk to and from school with their hands behind their backs. I knew nothing about sex offenders, but I figured I would find out soon enough.

THE TOUR

John closed the school doors, and we headed down the hallway to his office. His office had an old wooden desk at one end and a long meeting table that took up the rest of the space. The wall of windows allowed a view of the gym and a large sports field for the boys. We chatted about what he was looking for in a vice principal. He expressed that he knew my background working in poverty-stricken schools in Portland. After about twenty minutes, he suggested we take a campus tour.

We stopped at the vocational training building and observed boys building birdhouses, welding, and learning how to use a measuring tape. They were busy working on projects, so we moved to the food services building. Huge vats of soup were being prepared, and a staff member was teaching boys how to decorate a cake.

An older Black man looked up, so we headed his way.

John introduced me as an applicant for the vice principal position at the school. The man looked at me and said, "You must really need a job to work here."

I was happy to move on because the food had a greasy smell that seemed to permeate through the walls.

Nearby was the area for participants in the secure intensive treatment program (SITP). Those having committed serious crimes such as murder were housed in this area. I didn't want to know the details of what kind of life they had locked away from their family and community. Boys in this area were mostly older than the ones living in the units near the campus entrance. They lived in individual cells, attended school in the area, and ate four to a table. They were having lunch later than the boys in the front living units.

I stopped at one of the tables to ask if they liked the food, and no one answered. "They are not allowed to talk while eating," answered a dining room staff supervisor.

A teacher was assigned to the school located in the SITP unit. Boys in SITP were not allowed to attend any programs on the other part of the campus. They ate, slept, went to school, shot hoops, and did their treatment in this one area of campus. I found the situation depressing and thought, *I would not want to be a teacher in this unit.* It was time to move on.

As we left the area, I glanced at a boy sitting quietly. He looked up at me, and a smile broke out. Little did I know that I would see him again in different circumstances.

"Well, what do you think?" I could tell John hoped to get a yes out of me.

"John, I must tell you that these seem like the students I taught in the public schools; they just got in trouble, and now they are here. I could come back tomorrow and stand in the hallways while the students moved to and from their classes." I picked up my notepad and headed out of the area as John walked alongside to see me to the facility's exit. We agreed on 8:45 a.m. during the first class change for my return the next day.

Once outside, I looked back while getting my handbag out of the car trunk. Some boys were playing basketball beside their living unit while two staff sat in plastic chairs supervising.

After my visit had ended, I started thinking about my teaching days at a new experimental school designed by Harvard graduate students. In the spring of 1967, the Portland Public Schools were invited to participate in a cooperative project to develop a more realistic secondary school curriculum. The group of experienced teachers and administrators working for doctorates at Harvard University presented their ideas for improving the secondary school curriculum. Their objectives included designing an educational program relevant to the needs and interests of all adolescents, providing more opportunities for students to explore adult roles, familiarizing themselves with the world of work, and creating a democratic sense of community within the school. Some of what I learned did not come from any textbook.

One former student came to mind. The class was typing, and he was given little notice when he came to the class late. He came to me and said, "I found this baby kitten last night while I was out late. Could we nap in the back of the room?" *How could I say anything but yes?* When class was over, I asked him to leave the kitten until the end of the school day; he could then take it home with him. The kitten slept on a towel in a sink in the classroom. I was hoping the student wasn't homeless, as many are, since their bad homelife often causes them to be homeless and find a new place to live.

Driving back to the correctional facility the next day, I felt more comfortable knowing what to expect. Or did I?

John met me, and we chatted while waiting for the bell to ring for a class change. The students started pouring out of the classrooms and library, but they were not silent. Some were laughing, and others glared at classmates as they passed each other. A few had to be reminded to move on. Today, it was a little like a high school on the "outs." "Outs" describes the world outside of a correctional facility.

As we walked to the office area where a student had just been sent to the detention room, we stopped by to see what was happening. R. R. had written a note for Mr. Cassidy in the detention room. Mr. Cassidy read it out loud:

> *Today I walked into class and tried to do what the teacher told me and I felt she was targeting me but I told her I disrespect you and don't like you. Also feel you are targeting me and she said I hate you. I dislike your words can't exsplane how much I dislike you. It seems that you don't like me and I hate you and dislike you also. When I started I told her the only reason I will be nice too you is because I don't want to go to detission and at the end she said, I'm not going to take this go to detission and stay there!!!*

Mr. Cassidy asked R. R. to sit down and write two hundred times: I will not talk back to the teacher.

I glanced at what R. R. was writing as I was ready to leave. He wrote "I" 200 times and would be moving on to "will" 200 times.

The teachers had phones in their rooms to call for emergency backup. However, if a student was ordered to leave a classroom and go to detention, that was better than getting angry and being hauled off to a stricter detention room at the far end of campus near SITP.

When I visited classrooms, most teachers welcomed me and either continued their lesson or stopped to chat briefly.

I was given a small office with a window on the top half of the door. I could look out the window and see the office staff working on their daily tasks. A lot of what they had to do was see what a student at the main office window needed. It could be to see the doctor or sign a "blue slip," referring to the color of the paper, indicating they would soon be going home.

On my second day on the job, a lot happened, so I stayed after everyone had left at 4 p.m. I wanted to plan for the next day without interruptions, and I thought about teachers who had made a difference in my life. The teachers I remember are the ones who found something positive in each student, sometimes just saying something like: *You have the determination to figure out how to solve a particular problem*. The teachers allowing students to be part of the decision-making process was invaluable.

2

The Human-Animal Bond

Winter 1991

BOYS MUST ATTEND HIGH SCHOOL

Since many of the boys were dropouts of public schools, they didn't like that they were required to earn a high school diploma while incarcerated. The judges made it a strict order.

Teachers had not yet returned from their winter break. The students could spend time at the gym, and volunteers brought special food to the living units. A call had gone out to the list of volunteers about donating items that could be used by all youths in the living units. Some had received holiday gifts from family members or girlfriends. A visit was often made possible, which was usually a happy occasion to learn from those outside corrections what was happening in the community. Each unit had a special meal prepared by the campus food service.

DISMAL TEST SCORES

I reviewed student files and found that many of the incarcerated boys had deficient scores on the nationally used California Achievement Test (CAT). Many of the students had dropped out of public schools before entering MacLaren. They were only attending school and were required to earn a high school diploma because it was a requirement for their release from incarceration conditions.

I was determined to help them succeed and wracked my brain trying to figure out how to hook these boys into finishing high school. They responded poorly to traditional teaching methods, so I knew innovation was called for. Since many youths were visual learners and often wanted to come to the school office to pet the resident cat brought in by a staff member, I wondered if a human-animal bonding offering might be worth considering.

We did have a cat on campus, but he usually hung out in the lobby of the administration building. I had noticed him being friendly when small children visited on Sundays. There had been attempts to place the cat elsewhere, but he was unwilling to leave the campus. He had wandered from an area where local farmers grew vegetables to sell at roadside stands. The youth named the cat Fred MacLaren, and he became the mascot because the youth said he spread cheer and inner peace to everyone he greeted. Fred was even nominated Employee of the Month. The tabby blue-eyed cat was a winner.

My first pet was a yellow cat named Bruce. We lived in Panama at the time, where my dad worked on the naval base. While all of us kids loved Bruce, I spent more time with him than my siblings. I told him my secrets and carried on many one-sided conversations with him that he listened to with what I took to be absolute interest. My parents didn't let him inside, but I dashed outside to see him every morning before the school bus arrived. He usually waited for me when I returned from school later in the day.

When I was in the fifth grade, my dad announced, without argument or discussion, that we were headed to California. We barely had time to say goodbye to our friends, and I was sad to leave my favorite teacher, Miss Baird.

On the day of our departure, we arose before the sun. We were to take what we could carry with us on the plane. Items we could carry had been laid out on a table at the entrance of our home. I chose a small book—*As You Like It* by William Shakespeare. I could not read it, but I liked that it

Fred, the blue-eyed striped cat, lived on campus. (Photo from author's collection.)

was small and easy to carry. As we readied to leave, my dad lined us up on the porch, and there was my yellow cat, Bruce. I picked him up.

"Leave him be. It's time to get in the car," my dad bellowed. My dad ignored my cries.

As we drove away, tears slipped down my cheeks. I feared that without me to care for him, Bruce would either starve or be the victim of a catfight.

My thoughts were soon interrupted when John stopped by to see how I was doing.

I expressed my concern about poor educational outcomes and trauma in the homes of many of the students. John's response was, "That's why I hired you. You will figure out what to do."

RESEARCH FINDINGS

Stories of the amazing bonds between people and their dogs fascinate even the most pragmatic people.

It was therapist Boris Levinson's two books, *Pet-Oriented Child Psychotherapy* (1969) and *Pets and Human Development* (1972), that launched serious study and research on the human-animal bond. The term *human-animal bond* was coined by Leo K. Bustad, DVM, when he offered a lecture series called the "Human-Pet Relationship" in the early 1980s at the Human-Pet Relationship International Symposium in Vienna.

I was familiar with the work done by the Delta Society (now Pet Partners), and Dr. Bustad was one of the founding members. The Delta Society's extensive research showed the healing power of human-animal bonds. Could that bond also help with education? Could it motivate students to look forward to coming to school? What practical educational skills could it enhance? The more I thought about it and observed the students, the more the idea grew on me. The connection between incarcerated boys and dogs considered unadoptable in shelters was clear. Both were populations people preferred out of sight. Neglected and alone, problems increased, and the likelihood of a positive outcome was unlikely. Many people do not tolerate a youth who commits crimes or a dog who acts out. Lock up the boy. Kill the dog.

Since I was new to corrections, I sought input from teachers. I learned that some boys had a long history of delinquency, poor academic skills, little or no work experience, and a lack of confidence in their abilities.

Additionally, a high percentage of the boys came from dysfunctional families with multiple problems, including poverty, drug and alcohol abuse, criminal backgrounds, joblessness, lack of education, and so forth. Many families had only one parent, and that one parent often had a series of partners. Some of the boys came from more typical middle-class families and had rebelled against parents they thought were too strict.

Every youth had a juvenile corrections intake file with treatment goals such as continuing education, developing empathy for victims, dealing with gang issues, and avoiding criminal thinking errors. It was not unusual for a youth to have as many as twenty past referrals from violations. The file also included family background, prior out-of-home placements, school history, employment history, substance use and abuse, a medical/psychiatric/psychological report, and recommendations.

MacLaren's population had an age range between twelve and twenty-five, with an average age of approximately sixteen and a half years. They were incarcerated for a wide variety of crimes, up to and including murder, rape, sodomy, kidnapping, and arson. Many of the youth failed in community placement attempts, requiring a return to custody, with a significant number failing repeatedly. At this time, more than 350 boys and young men were serving sentences at MacLaren.

Some of MacLaren's juvenile offenders came from families where pets were disposed of frequently. Such information came from family history in intake files and from the youth themselves. These juveniles never learned the responsibility and care of a pet. However, I began learning that some even bonded with a pair of praying mantises found on campus and housed in an aquarium in one of the living units. For some juveniles, this was their first bonding experience with animals. They had found a living creature they could trust, one who would not abuse them.

Further encouraged, I set out to find if any existing programs in corrections included dogs. I found there were at least sixteen prisons (more exist today) in which animals in a correctional facility were housed to help inmates who were depressed, troubled, or in need of vocational training. Such programs reported positive behavioral changes in the inmates and better contact between staff and inmates. They increased caring and vocational skills such as dog grooming, obedience training, and animal career skills. None of these programs were in a juvenile correctional facility.

When I lived in New York, I visited Green Chimneys in Brewster and liked how the founder, Dr. Sam Ross, incorporated dogs and other animals into the learning lessons for young children. I studied programs such as Purdy Women's Prison; Gig Harbor; Washington State, a puppy raiser program; PAL in Washington, D.C., founded by Earl Strimple, DVM, a hands-on animal care program for at-risk youth residing in the inner city; and HALT in Knoxville, Tennessee, a program for at-risk adolescents and dogs from shelters. Others who graciously and willingly shared their knowledge and expertise were Earl Strimple, DVM, and Lynette Hart, DVM.

Armed with the firm belief that pairing unwanted dogs and incarcerated youth could help both, I began creating a plan to set up a program. I began talking about the possibility of such a program to various staff, administrators, and youth, seeking support for my idea.

After nearly two years of research and brainstorming, I presented my initial plan to MacLaren administrators Rick Hill, Robert Jester, and John Pendergrass. I had done my research well and knew I would encounter at least some strong opposition, so I needed to cement their support before proceeding.

Correctional facilities are known for being no-nonsense, punishment-oriented institutions focused on keeping communities safe. Such institutions are not quick to embrace nontraditional programs behind the walls. Especially if the dogs are going to live on-site 24/7.

3

Do We Want a Dog Program?

Fall and Spring 1992

Many teachers and educators have implemented programs to inspire young people to succeed despite poverty, lack of parental or other adult support, and a poor start in school, which can leave them lagging. Some successful programs include after-school tutoring, summer school, and Big Sister and Big Brother programs, which provide extended mentorship.

Few programs had ever been tested in juvenile corrections, so I knew I had to devise something innovative from scratch. I had submitted an initial plan to the MacLaren administration. I knew much more planning would be needed because I envisioned an on-site program.

I thought back to teachers and others who had influenced me. I kept returning to animals I had loved and to how they had seen me through tough times at home because somebody loved me unconditionally—as I loved them.

I began to put more and more thought into creating a program at MacLaren where boys and shelter dogs could help each other. I shared ideas with John, the principal, daily in hopes he would strongly advocate for the program with other administrators. Selected boys and hard-to-place shelter dogs would work together to achieve successful outcomes. Two different populations could help each other. Both groups had been neglected—both needed help. The priority would be selecting dogs with behavioral problems and ones in a shelter for the longest period.

My idea met with what I'll call cautious optimism. Robert Jester was open to the concept but wanted more information before committing. This was quite reasonable. Encouraged that my idea had been met with interest instead of dismissal, I formulated a more formal plan with the help of the school principal and a committee of school staff interested in the concept.

QUESTIONS AND CONCERNS

First, though, I needed to address safety and security issues. I met with security staff to learn their concerns and what I needed to know about keeping myself safe, since I was new to corrections and would often be alone at the far end of campus.

I talked with more people on campus. Some were highly enthusiastic and some were adamantly against my idea, with the majority falling in between. Everyone agreed that many questions had to be answered and that there were a lot of issues that would have to be considered. Who would run the program? Where would the dogs live? How many boys would be chosen? Where would the dogs come from? How would it be funded? What were the goals? How would success be measured? Planning also involved the ideal profile of participants, gleaned by consulting with corrections staff to determine what type of individual would be successful when working with the dogs.

When excited about an innovative program, it is easy to forget that not everyone shares the same vision for moving forward. Gaining support from people with the power to make decisions proved extremely important. Since the high school was under the umbrella of the corrections administration, I would have to get approval from administrators to start the program. I checked in again with Superintendent Jester to discuss the idea further. He was a good listener and encouraged me to continue considering all the logistics of starting such a program. I wondered why he wasn't jumping up and down in agreement with my idea. He brought up a situation with a Saint Bernard in SITP. Two boys got into a fistfight, and when security tried to break it up, the dog intervened in favor of the boys.

Several days later, Superintendent Jester came to the school to talk with me. He said, "There is a boy in lockup for manslaughter because he shot someone who shot his dog. What if we start with him?" I was happy to learn I was approved to start with one boy.

His name was Anthony, and he lived in SITP, where the boys considered the state's most violent offenders were housed. The next day, I went to SITP to meet him. I soon found out the whole story.

Anthony's eyes took on a faraway look as he recounted the incident:

Gross and me was just being stupid drunk kids fighting like dumb boys will do, but Sinbad, my pit bull didn't take it that way. He thought we was in a serious altercation and he jumped Gross. Having a pit bull jump you is serious stuff, but that's no excuse for Gross pulling out his gun and shooting Sinbad. That was just wrong.

The stupid thing is, Gross and I didn't have any issues. I'd been in a gang before, but our fight didn't have nothing to do with that. I wasn't even in a gang anymore. I got out of that to start selling drugs. Gross and me was just two little boys with too much alcohol in them so we'd started fighting and next thing I know, my dog is shot. I had an anger problem to begin with and somebody shooting my dog and saying he'd kill me too just filled me with rage like you wouldn't believe.

I carried my dog to my house. He was bleeding like crazy, covering me with blood. I was soaked with it. I thought for sure he was going to die in my arms. Know what they say about your dog being your best friend? Well, it was true. So I got Sinbad home and cleaned him up and made him comfortable. I gave him a big bowl of water cause he'd just lost all that blood and then I went in my house and ran upstairs and got my gun. I kept it under my mattress. It was a revolver that I got from the neighborhood. We all had guns. It cost fifty dollars, so it wasn't any great thing, but it was what I had. I jumped on my bike and went out to even the score.

A friend saw me and rode up to join me. He was twelve. I was fifteen, but that didn't matter. We knew each other and he was on my side. He couldn't believe somebody shot my dog.

I found Gross a couple of blocks from his house. He was surrounded by all these friends of his, acting like he was some kind of hero for shooting a gun. Like that wasn't something we'd all done before. We was in gangs. We was just drunk and arguing and my dog took it all wrong.

Gross saw us coming and saw my gun and grabbed a friend and tried to hide behind him, thinking he'd be safe or something, but I was too drunk and mad to care who I hit. I fired a couple of times to get people to back off. Which they did.

When it came down to Gross and me, I just got up close and fired. He went down. I fired four more times, thinking of Sinbad and how he could die and how he'd never done a single thing to deserve to get shot at. He was protecting me, just like I'd taught him to do.

When I saw Gross wasn't breathing or moving anymore, I threw the gun down on top of him and got on my bike. It all turned surreal then, like something in a movie. Everything started moving in slow motion and the only thing that was clear to me was the sound of a lawn mower.

It was so weird that there was somebody dead, and he was out there mowing his lawn without a care in the world. But he must have figured out what was going on because next thing I know he's heading for his house, and I see him on the phone. Drunk or not, I wasn't stupid. I knew he was calling 911 and I'd better get out of there quick.

So, I pedaled as fast as I could. I remember hitting a curb and almost going down, but I got my balance again. I rode over to this store where an older friend worked, and I told him how I'd just done something crazy.

He said to put my bike in back of his truck. He took me over to a friend's house, the guy I was selling drugs for him. He lived in Seattle, but he was in Portland for a few days. He tried to calm me down, but basically, he didn't want me there in case the cops came; they might come down on him, too, and he didn't need the hassle.

I understood. So, I went to my girlfriend's house. She was a lot older than me. Twenty-four.

I stayed there for the night and when I got sober, I couldn't believe what I'd done. I didn't know what to do.

The next morning, I saw myself on the news. I couldn't even think straight, couldn't make sense of what a stupid thing I'd done. I didn't have any problems with Gross. We got along just fine and now he was dead on account of me.

I went back to talk to the friend from the store. I called my mom from there, and my friend, my mom, and I went to the police station so I could turn myself in.

I couldn't believe what a mess I'd made of things. I'd been running with the wrong people for a long time, since I was a little kid. I'd shot at people before and done bad stuff, but I'd gotten out of gangs and wanted to start over. At least the violence. I didn't want any more of that.

I'd gone up to Seattle to live with the guy I was selling drugs for to get away from the old gang stuff, but my mom wanted me back in Portland to go to school. She was a good mom. She had it tough, too. She was always working to try to make ends meet. My dad wasn't anywhere around, and my mom married another guy who I didn't like. He ended up getting shot and killed. She didn't want my life to be that way.

So, I came back to Portland like she wanted me to and before the day was even over, I'd killed a friend, and my dog was all messed up because he'd been shot.

Anthony became Project POOCH's first participant. The program name stood for "Positive Opportunities—Obvious Change with Hounds." His records at MacLaren described him as a well-spoken, friendly student who had shown improvement since his incarceration a little over a year ago. His test scores were average, and he had not been involved in any altercations while at MacLaren.

As abhorrent as his crime was, Anthony impressed me, and I knew he was exactly the kind of boy who fit the criteria for a POOCH participant. He had demonstrated his love for dogs. He served as an example of taking responsibility for his actions, even though it meant he would be incarcerated. His background made him quick to anger. I believed childhood issues could be addressed by caring for a dog. I could not imagine a more ideal first participant to join POOCH to benefit from the healing power of the human-animal bond. I could relate to Anthony's story.

MY CHILDHOOD

As I headed back to the main school building, an incident with my childhood dog surfaced in my memory.

One day, my dad came home from work at the mill with a surprise. It was a yellow, rambunctious puppy. We named him Bugsy. Bugsy was the closest thing to affection I had experienced. My parents rarely hugged us. (My dad hugged me when I graduated college.)

When my dad got his monthly paycheck, we would go into town to purchase groceries. Bugsy tried to follow but soon gave up and went back home. Bugsy was waiting in the unfenced front yard when we returned from shopping. He had killed four chickens that my dad had recently purchased.

My dad was furious. My mother herded us into the house. She pulled the blind closed as my dad walked off with his rifle on his shoulder and Bugsy by his side with his tail wagging.

Nobody ever said a word about the execution. I hated my dad for what he had done. I still tear up today as I write about this part of growing up in a home where animals were disposable.

Since I was familiar with MacLaren's popular building trades offerings, I met with the staff about involving the boys in building a dog kennel. Freddie Mitchell would be the staff leader to help determine materials needed and cost, but we had yet to decide where the kennel would be located on the nearly one hundred acres of the campus.

I also helped plan a nationwide human-animal bond conference to be held in Portland. One of the presenters scheduled to speak was Dr. Sam Ross, the founder of Green Chimneys in Brewster, New York. I contacted Dr. Ross and asked if he could visit the MacLaren campus and advise me on the best location for a kennel. I was giddy with happiness—what better person could advise me as we looked at the pros and cons of various possible locations? We decided the best place would be between the main high school building and the building trades area. This would allow dogs to view students as they moved back and forth from building to building. It would also allow students not in the program to interact with the dogs.

I enjoyed watching the progress and how all the building trades students planned to build something that was needed. The dogs would also need dog houses to get out of the rain, which was suggested by one of the students. A team of students asked an instructor if he could find plans for building dog houses. The students were learning math by measuring and how to install insulation along with painting the houses. They were thinking about the dogs as they planned the houses. The houses had to be elevated off the ground to stay warmer, and removable roofs would allow for easier cleaning. Someone suggested they install plexiglass windows so the dogs could see out. They weren't just building; they were thinking through what the consequences would be for the decisions they were making.

Boys learn how to build wooden dog houses. (Photo from author's collection.)

CARING TEACHERS

Most of the boys had no father involved in their lives, so the building trades staff took on that role as they demonstrated how to plan and build the dog houses and the kennel area. Some had never used a measuring tape or a hammer until the dog kennel project was presented as a learning project that could provide skills needed in construction or building. Staff member Pete Grigorieff brought in his rottweiler to try out the dog houses for size. Everyone had a short work stoppage to meet the dog.

4

Training Boys, Training Dogs

Summer 1992

Anthony was permitted to move from SITP to Lord High School, where boys from the front living units attended school. I stopped by the art class to update Anthony on when we would get the first dog. He was drawing the likeness of a pit bull. He showed a lot of talent. I asked if he would be interested in drawing the logo for Project POOCH.

He did not hesitate. He looked at his art teacher for approval, and she allowed him to proceed with his drawing. After he completed the logo and I registered it with the U.S. Trademark Office, I had $50 deposited into his trust account, which every youth had set up for them when they came to MacLaren. Since he had done incredible work on the logo, I asked if he would like to design the program cover for the Project POOCH grand opening. He said, "The POOCH program makes me feel real. Sometimes, being locked up, I don't feel real."

FUNDING, STAFFING, AND HOUSING DOGS

Jean Vollum had given us $10,000 in 1992, which was in a restricted fund for kennel expenses. She was born in Calgary, Alberta, and married Howard Vollum, founder of Tektronix in Portland, Oregon. Jean loved music, the arts, animals, and the environment. She was a caring philanthropist who shared what she had with those around her. The program was moving in a positive direction. However, I knew there would continue to be obstacles and issues as we worked to develop the program. Never giving up hope was my motto.

THE FIRST DOG ARRIVES

Catherine, a special education teacher experienced in working with and training dogs, had gone to the Oregon Humane Society and teamed up with the education director, Carol Shiveley, to select the first dog for the program. I told Catherine to look for a dog with minor behavioral problems to give Anthony an incentive to work so the dog would be adoptable. I thought changing a dog's bad behavior to good behavior would encourage Anthony to look at his own behavior.

Catherine and Carol agreed: "Let's go for the energetic Labrador retriever." The dog was about sixty pounds and untrained. His family gave him up because he was "too energetic." When Catherine returned to MacLaren with the first dog to enroll in Project POOCH, she asked Anthony to come outside his classroom to meet the dog. The first thing the dog did was jump up on Anthony to greet him. Anthony laughed and said, "Patience." (Patience is the second word in the POOCH mission statement.)

I wanted to involve all the students, so I announced a "Name the Dog Contest." The prize would be candy and soda in the canteen. The winning name was Grover, the name of one of the living units. I suspected that everyone in the Grover living unit voted for the name.

Anthony had yet to earn his high school diploma. He was taking needed classes in high school and earning school credit in communications and careers by working with Grover. Every morning, Anthony hurried to Grover's dog run next to a small shelter constructed by the building trades students. The shelter provided a warm place to sleep and store dog food, bowls, balls, and leashes. He leashed Grover and let him sniff around the fenced area next to a large oak tree so that he could clean the run.

Catherine had large dogs that she bred and showed at dog shows. She was gentle and calm, teaching Anthony to get his dog to sit before being leashed. She then continued teaching as she and Anthony walked with Grover around campus. Getting Grover to keep from pulling when he saw squirrels took a while, but Anthony was eager to learn. Seeing the first youth and dog having fun and freedom being out in the open air brought smiles.

Not too long after Grover's arrival, Anthony came to me and asked, "How soon can we get another dog to keep Grover company?" His voice turned sad as he added, "Grover is lonely being the only dog."

I reminded him I had promised the superintendent that we would start with one dog and work out any issues before adding to the program, but Anthony didn't want to let it go. He challenged me with, "Vernon likes dogs

First boy and first dog who started Project POOCH. (Photo from author's collection.)

and wants to be in the program." I was impressed by how he spoke up to advocate for Vernon, a fellow student, and the program.

"Let me think about it," I said.

I returned to Superintendent Jester to find out his thoughts about adding a second dog and a second boy. I also wanted to be transparent and reassured him that I planned to keep my word about one dog and boy until he agreed to expand the program.

A SECOND BOY JOINS THE PROGRAM

Jester had a heart for young people and wanted them to succeed so they would not return to MacLaren School for Boys. He agreed that Vernon could learn from the program.

I knew nothing about Vernon and needed to check out his background. He wasn't from Oregon. He had been hanging out with some friends with cars in his home state of Kansas. They hatched a plan to drive and commit petty crimes to pay their way across the country. Vernon and his friends ended up in Oregon, where they got caught in a robbery.

Since Anthony was ahead on dog training, he wanted Vernon to have a dog with some training. Anthony took on the role of helping Vernon take responsibility for Grover, which worked out great. The two had similar personalities—easygoing, willing to learn, and able to show patience with each other and Grover.

Catherine returned to the humane society and chose a Border collie/Aussie mix as the second dog to join the program. The transfer of Grover to Vernon took place after Catherine gave her approval. She told Vernon that if he couldn't care for the dog, it would be his responsibility to arrange staff to call the kennel, giving Vernon full responsibility.

Anthony named the second dog Spirit because the dog would be his spirit guide.

After both dogs had been in the program a while, Anthony said, "The dogs smell and need baths." We didn't have a tub.

"How are you going to solve the problem?" I asked.

They started looking for a water source and realized that they already had what they needed because the dog shelter had a hose hooked up nearby that they had been using for cleaning out the dog runs every morning.

We didn't have dog shampoo, so I went to the nearby farm store during lunchtime, where I found shampoo for almost every kind of farm animal, including a wide selection for dogs.

Anthony and Vernon had given the dogs a long walk around campus in the morning and were ready to get to work bathing them after lunch. Before returning to their living units for lunch, the dogs were put in their runs, which had insulated dog houses built by the building trades students.

After lunch, Anthony and Vernon took the dogs for another walk around campus. Then they got busy shampooing Grover and Spirit. One boy would hold a dog while the other applied shampoo and then rinsed the dog with water from the hose. I started considering raising money for a professional dog groomer and other needed supplies. I had no idea where a tub could be installed if we were to get a dog groomer to teach us how to bathe and groom a dog.

Catherine was spending increasingly more of her time with the dogs. She helped Anthony and Vernon develop a daily routine: dog walks around campus, cleaning, playing, feeding, and basic dog training. She also helped them develop humane training skills (no choke chains or pinch collars) until we could get a dog trainer. She had been hired to prepare individual education plans for special needs students. She was needed away from the kennel and in the school since many of the incarcerated boys needed IEPs.

Spirit, a black-and-white Border collie/Aussie mix, was the second dog in the program. (Photo from author's collection.)

FINDING A DOG TRAINER

On my way to MacLaren every morning, I passed a dog boarding kennel, so I stopped to ask if they could recommend a dog trainer. The boarding kennel was operated by an older couple who bred and showed small dogs at dog shows.

When I explained Project POOCH and how the program needed a dog trainer, JoAnn (co-owner of the boarding kennel) said, "I am a 4-H dog club trainer and can help you out." I wanted to hug her. Just a half mile from MacLaren, I found a dog trainer. She was willing to volunteer her time immediately but could only come once a week. She could teach basics: come, sit, stay, leave it, and walk on a loose leash. Introducing house training was another skill she would add to the lessons.

Anthony and Vernon needed a dog trainer who could come more than one day a week, so I asked a friend for recommendations.

Kevin was a young dog trainer willing to come one day a week; however, he wanted to be paid for his time and gas money. We had small donations from supporters to pay him for a while. (JoAnn was donating her time.)

Now with two dog trainers. Anthony and Vernon would receive expert guidance two days a week. Mission accomplished. I crossed the task off my list. I also liked having a male role model for the dog handlers. Kevin brought his German shepherd to demonstrate the skills of a well-trained dog. His dog gave Anthony and Vernon hope that they could do the same with their dogs.

Looking at background files was important in selecting appropriate boys for the program. No boys with animal abuse and/or bestiality in their background would be considered. As I read the files, I found that many boys had no father in the home. Some of them had never even met their biological father. One boy's file read: Child Protective Services has maintained care and custody of this boy for most of his entire life. His biological father's parental rights were terminated because he was never involved in his children's lives. The mother's parental rights were also terminated. The boy has been in over thirty Child Protective Services placements and several abusive foster care homes.

The boy's behavior in foster care was difficult to manage due to the emotional damage he experienced as a young boy. His behavior was self-destructive, impulsive, and hyperactive. He had been on prescribed drugs since the age of six to help stabilize his aggressive behavior. Psychological examinations diagnosed him as severely emotionally disturbed due to the abuse he had suffered. According to the boy, his mother heavily used illegal narcotics. He soon ran from his mother's home and was homeless. He estimated that he had stolen ten automobiles. He was then committed to MacLaren School for Boys. He was assessed for special education services at MacLaren and required special help in math and reading.

After discussing the boy's background with Catherine, she agreed he could be helped by participation in the dog program. Also, two dog trainers could give more individualized help to those needing it. However, with two dog trainers, it was not long before I saw a few problems. There was a large open field between the building trades classes and the high school where JoAnn would help Anthony and Vernon train Grover and Spirit. I heard her say, "Bring the bitch over for me to look at her." The bitch she was referring to was Spirit.

Since arriving at MacLaren, I learned quickly that some adult and juvenile males used inappropriate language when referring to females. I would have none of it. I marched over to JoAnn and instructed her not to use the word "bitch" when talking about a female dog because I was trying to teach males that it was not appropriate to refer to females as bitches. She came right back at me and informed me that was the word used by dog breeders.

"That may be," I said. "However, please do not use the term when working with the boys in the program."

Additionally, Grover did not take to obedience training as quickly as we had hoped, so JoAnn said, "Grover needs me to take him home and show him a thing or two to straighten him out."

"No, Grover can't leave campus," I replied. I went on to explain that one of the things I hoped the boys in the program would learn was patience. Grover could be the test case. Her body language let me know she disagreed. In retrospect, maybe she and I could have had a private conversation out of the earshot of the youth.

Kevin, our other trainer, arrived later in the week with his well-trained German shepherd, which continued to impress Anthony and Vernon. During training sessions, the dog would calmly take a down position under a nearby shade tree and ignore the POOCH dogs.

JoAnn asked the boys why they were training their dogs a certain way the following week.

Anthony spoke up: "This is how Kevin taught us to do it."

The fight was on. The two trainers did not approve of the other person's training methods, and they let it be known. My well-thought-out plan of having two trainers was not successful. JoAnn left.

Kevin continued but wasn't willing to continue indefinitely without being paid more due to the distance he had to drive to get to MacLaren. I asked him to stay on through the upcoming grand opening, promising I would see if I could find a way to increase his pay.

5

Grand Opening

1993

Anthony and Vernon needed very little supervision. They liked working with the dogs and knew a mess-up would end the program and put them back in their living units. It was time to send a press release and inform the public that incarcerated boys can make good things happen for themselves and the dogs they save.

OFFICIAL PRESS RELEASE

Project POOCH (Positive Opportunities—Obvious Change with Hounds) is the first Human-Animal Resident program in Juvenile Corrections in the United States. The Project was introduced to the public on June 2, 1993.

Five months later, the first dog (Grover) has passed his obedience test and will be adopted by an approved family at a ceremony at MacLaren School, October 21, 1993, 11:30 a.m., dog kennel area or, if raining, school library.

Grover and his MacLaren student handler will demonstrate what they have learned by working with dog obedience trainers, a veterinarian, and humane society personnel.

Project POOCH is a Human-Animal bonding project that teaches selected participants Responsibility, Patience, and Compassion for All Life. Participants can tell guests what they have learned about proper pet care and training, and the dogs will demonstrate their unconditional love for the students.

Project POOCH is a joint demonstration project with the Delta Society, an international organization (later changed to Pet Partners) that studies people, animals, and the environment. The project aims to rehabilitate juvenile offenders at MacLaren School by training and caring for unwanted dogs from the Oregon Humane Society.

Funding is by the Autzen Foundation, Samuel S. Johnson Foundation, and anonymous donors.

Jean Vollum funded the program with $10,000 for the structure and dog enclosures.

Ceremony at MacLaren School for Boys
2630 North Pacific Hwy.
Woodburn, Oregon
October 21, 1993
11:30 a.m.

THE FIRST DOG ADOPTED

Finally, the big day arrived. Excitement was in the air after months of planning, learning, raising funds, and finding the right boys and dogs.

Anthony and Vernon were a little concerned. Vernon had taught Grover how to shake and roll over; however, the dog's bad habit of jumping on people to greet them was not always extinguished. To get Grover ready for the event, he received much special attention; he went on long walks around the campus. I was cautiously optimistic that he would behave. It was a mild fall day at the correctional facility. The television crew was busy setting up as a few guests showed up.

Boys from the building trades who had built the dog enclosures were seated so their faces would not show on television because there is a protocol regarding confidentiality due to their young ages. Anthony and Vernon had signed release forms, so they were cleared to be interviewed by the film crew.

Linda Hines, director of the Delta Society, and Dale Dunning, director of the Oregon Humane Society, also were interviewed. A staff member was there to adopt Grover. Carol Shiveley, education director of the Oregon Humane Society, and Superintendent Robert Jester spoke.

I had stayed up the night before baking cookies shaped like dog bones. Each one had green frosting on the top. Baking six dozen large, bone-shaped cookies with green frosting took the better part of the evening. Still, I smiled when I thought it appropriate to have dog bone cookies for the grand opening of the first on-site dog program in a juvenile correctional setting.

Superintendent Jester welcomed everyone and put a positive spin on the first-ever dog program.

Linda Hines spoke and shared research about dog programs in adult prisons. She noted, "Such programs soften hardened hearts." She congratulated Anthony and Vernon for training Grover so he would be ready for adoption.

Grover was clean, and his teeth were brushed. He seemed increasingly excited as the sound system needed adjusting and people moved around.

It was then my turn to introduce Grover's first handler, Anthony. I looked over at him. He was looking down at the ground as I spoke.

"Anthony has worked consistently every day and showed a lot of patience to get a pass for Grover when it came time to take the required Canine Good Citizen test. Anthony, will you please bring Grover out of his dog run to meet his adopter?"

A television reporter was standing near Grover's dog run as he was being leashed. Grover got excited to get to Vernon and jumped up on the reporter, causing her to fall to the ground. Everyone froze.

After everything settled down, I again asked Anthony to bring Grover over and put him on a sit. Vernon helped in case Grover decided to act out again. As I spoke about the program, my voice started to tremble as memories of my dog, Bugsy, resurfaced—the long-ago memory of my dad walking off with his rifle over his shoulder and Bugsy happily walking beside him on the way to his death. I had to get my bearings, or I would burst into tears. I quickly pulled my attention back to Anthony and Vernon. Vernon was about to show what he had taught Grover before handing the leash to Rick, the adopter. As Rick led Grover away from the event, Vernon walked right behind them. When Rick and Grover turned around the corner of the administration building, Vernon returned with a sad look.

The television crew began getting sound bites about how Anthony and Vernon felt about Grover's adoption. Anthony was happy that Grover got a home, but Vernon said, "It's okay."

Another boy who wasn't in the program came walking by and stopped. The next thing I knew, he was being interviewed by the cameraman with the television crew. He was asked, "What do you know about dogs?" The boy responded, "I know that at first, you must learn to control yourself before you can control a dog."

RECEPTION IN THE SCHOOL LIBRARY

It was time for the reception with cookies and juice in the school library. A staff member escorted the building trades students to the library ahead of the guests so we could easily track them. They were seated four at a table with a plate of dog bone cookies I had baked in the center.

As I walked to the reception with the guests, I encouraged them to sit at tables with the boys and ask questions about their work building the area for the dogs. As we entered the library, I was shocked to discover the boys had eaten all the cookies placed on the tables. I didn't see that one coming. I had no cookies in reserve for the guests.

When the television crew finally left the facility, I breathed a sigh of relief.

With Grover's adoption, I was concerned when Vernon did not show up at the dog area the next day. When I asked why he didn't come he referred to Grover's adoption when he answered, "I didn't know it could go so deep." I convinced him to come back and continue in the program.

Spirit was now the only dog in the program. Vernon wanted a dog.

ANTHONY AND VERNON VISIT THE HUMANE SOCIETY

To my surprise, Superintendent Jester arranged for a correctional officer (CO), along with Anthony and Vernon, to go to the humane society to pick out another dog.

Several hours after Anthony and Vernon left to go to the humane society, the school secretary informed me they were on their way back. Shortly after, the principal came to my office bearing disturbing news. A man had been at the humane society looking at dogs while Anthony and Vernon had been there. The man discovered his wallet missing and insisted two "Black boys" took it because no one else was around.

I told John, "I know they didn't take the man's wallet."

When the boys returned, a staff member searched them and confirmed they had not taken the man's wallet. I felt so humiliated for Anthony and Vernon for being stripped and searched.

Another call came from the humane society: "The man found his wallet. He had misplaced it."

I was seething that the man had falsely accused Anthony and Vernon.

6

Troubling Times

1993–1994

While it was exciting to have the new program underway, we ran into unanticipated problems. Fortunately, solving them constantly improved the program.

ADOPTER RETURNS GROVER

A few days after Grover had been adopted, his adopter said he was bringing him back because he had dug holes in their newly landscaped backyard. Anthony and Vernon were disappointed when I told them, but they gladly welcomed Grover back.

"Since you have learned a lot in the program, I would like to involve you in selecting another boy to join the team," I told them.

Catherine developed an application to select boys to join the program. The application helped determine if the boy should be granted a live group interview. (Anthony and Vernon joined the program by being interviewed without an application.)

SAMPLE APPLICATION

Name: Eduardo, Living Unit: McKay [I did not change how Eduardo wrote the answers.]

Question 1: Why would you like to work with a school dog? *Answer:* I would like very much to work with a dog in Project POOCH. I have always loved animals and I know working with them is a lot of fun. I also plan that someday I will be a veterinarian assistant, so this learning experience will help me a lot.

Question 2: My experience with dogs in my home? *Answer:* I have always had a dog even when I was little.

Question 3: How long will you probably be at MacLaren? *Answer:* Not sure.

Question 4: What do you already know about dogs? *Answer:* You got to have patience with them when trying to teach them something. I know that having an animal is a big responsibility. They look at their master for love and care.

Question 5: What would you like to learn about dogs? *Answer:* I would like to learn how to train dogs using different commands like walking on a leash, sitting, and how to lay.

The living unit manager and/or counselor must permit you to work in the dog program. Please have them sign below. You will be notified when to interview for POOCH in person. Please return your completed application to Ms. Dalton, vice principal.

If a boy was chosen for an interview, I made up a list of questions and sometimes had a dog nearby to observe the boy's reaction throughout the process. After the live interview, I reviewed the family history to ensure no animal abuse was in the records.

Eduardo became the third boy to work with the dogs. He did not have a lot of structure in his life before being sentenced to MacLaren. He said, "I was kicked out of school. I wouldn't say there was abuse, but I didn't have a very good childhood. I was molested when I was younger." He was fourteen when he came to MacLaren.

Anthony and Vernon showed him how to clean kennels and do other tasks for the dogs. Eduardo didn't have a dog immediately but already liked being in the program. He did not complain because he had no dog, but I knew he was ready.

Later that day, I talked with our math volunteer, Dirk, about the program. He shared that his wife was going into assisted living, and he planned on going with her. "They won't allow us to bring our little dog, Freckles, to live there," he said. There was silence until he asked, "Is there any chance you could take Freckles into the program?" I smiled. "I think we can do that." Freckles arrived the next day. Eduardo now had a dog.

WEEKEND STAFF NEEDED

I liked covering the program on Saturdays because I went to each living unit to pick up the dog handlers. It allowed them to share anything bothering them. Sometimes, they expressed frustration over staff telling them something like "restack the breakfast dishes" because they didn't stack them right the first time. Some might have hoped for a visit from family or a girlfriend. "I put on my best clothes and waited all afternoon, but no one came," said one boy.

When we arrived at the kennel, the boys were happy to see wagging tails and barking greetings from the dogs.

I decided to see if any teaching assistants would like to work Saturdays. Since their pay was low, there was a fair amount of interest. The school budget could handle extra pay for working Saturdays.

My free time on Saturdays did not last long. I started getting calls that the Saturday staff failed to show up. I would then head to the kennel to ensure the dogs were fed and exercised. When I asked the staff person why he did not show up on Saturday, he always had an excuse: "I got sick from something I ate Friday night," or "I stayed with my girlfriend, and she forgot to wake me up."

On Sundays, there was a regular staff member, Bob, from the recreation department. The boys in SITP got their required one-hour recreation daily. Bob would call Anthony and Vernon to take care of the dogs. They were reliable and trustworthy since they had been in the program for several months. Anthony sometimes had a visit, but Vernon had none.

Bob would leave them alone to take care of the dogs. After an hour, Bob came from SITP and returned Anthony and Vernon to their living units.

ROBERT THE ROOSTER MOVES IN

I was working late and noticed a white rooster with a bright red comb had settled in for the night on a horizontal bar along one of the classroom windows. I had no idea how many nights he had spent roosting on the bar. He decided to leave a nearby farm and spend his time at school.

The mostly white rooster flew onto campus and roosted at night on the bar outside the school window. (Photo from author's collection.)

The following day, I got a call that no one showed up to take the boys out to take care of the dogs. Once I arrived, I realized two of the boys had visits from family. I asked if I could take a couple of boys with good behavior records but not in the program. After a few basic instructions to the newbies, we headed to get the dogs out, walked, and fed.

Everyone soon had their dogs leashed and ready for a walk before being fed. I heard a boy yell, "Hey, Ms. D., come quick. Something has happened." I almost lost it as I got closer—Robert the rooster was dead. One of the boys said he had heard security talking about a rooster on the bar at the school. "The rooster had been hanging out at the school for about a month," he said.

"How did it happen?" asked one of the boys.

Another boy said, "When I went to get the dog out of her kennel, her door was slightly open. Since the dog was inside, I didn't think about it." Closer inspection showed a few white feathers in the dog's kennel space. I suspected the dog got out and worried the rooster to death by barking and lunging as Robert tried to stay on the bar. The boys wanted to give Robert a decent burial by the side of the school. I was not going to throw Robert in a garbage can. After all, "Compassion for all life" is part of our mission.

Memories of my chickens from childhood began to surface. I had bantam (also called banty) chickens in middle school. One day, I told my mother that something had happened to the female chicken, and all her babies except one were dead. I put the surviving chicken in a cardboard box with fabric on the top and placed it on the floor near my sleeping cot. When I woke up the next morning, there was no baby chicken. It was nowhere to be found until I looked under the blanket on my cot. It had jumped out of the box at night, and I had rolled on it. Dead. Tears came, and I felt guilty for not knowing how to keep the baby chicken safe. I wrapped it in a piece of velvet and put a cross on top before I buried it. I kept saying, "I'm sorry, I'm sorry."

Finally, I said to the dog handlers, "Let's do our dog walk, come back and feed the dogs, and then figure out what we need to do to prevent dogs from getting out in the future." They came up with an idea. They wanted me to go to the local farm store and buy latches so the dogs could not escape their outdoor spaces. "That is a great idea. I'll do it during lunch break," I said.

After they returned from lunch, the boys played with the dogs, practiced training commands, and put a latch on every dog gate. The dogs had dinner, and the boys took time to write in their journals about how the day went and any questions they had.

As I walked them back to their living units, we passed Robert's burial place; someone said, "Rest in peace." The boys demonstrated that, like humans, animals deserve a decent resting place after death.

Monday morning reminded me that not everyone on campus was excited about the program. I had hired a special education teacher to work with the boys daily, but the boys needed a supervised place to study dogs and write in their journals. Keeping a journal would not only help them track their progress, but it would also provide badly needed high school credit. The room I found was nothing grand, but it did have a desk, a settee, a chair, and a window so the office staff could supervise them.

When some teachers saw the boys in their new space in the school office area, they protested, mainly because the dogs were there. Yet the additional space improved the boys' ability to complete written assignments and work with their dogs simultaneously.

Finding curriculum materials for the high school age group was difficult, so I started developing my own with the help of well-known trainers such as Ian Dunbar, Jean Donaldson, and Patricia B. McConnell.

MISTREATMENT OF DOGS

A significant problem I had not foreseen was the mistreatment of dogs by boys not in the program. (There was a high standard for getting into the program.) While I expected the boys to interact with the dogs, perhaps even to befriend them and benefit from having dogs near the school, I had not considered that anyone would harm them. Yet, shortly after the dogs' arrival and curiosity waned, an office referral hit my desk, alerting me to a boy mistreating one of the dogs. I knew I had to approach this diplomatically. I could not allow this to go unaddressed. I acted quickly. I called the boy who had thrown sticks at Grover into my office. "Why did you throw a stick at Grover?" I asked. He said, "I just wanted Grover to stop barking."

"Have you considered looking at it from the dog's point of view?" I asked. "Grover is penned up, watching students pass from the main building to the vocational trades building. He barked because he had something to say to them. When you threw something at him, he had nowhere to go to feel safe." After discussing it for a while, the boy showed honest remorse. He promised not to do it again.

Anthony was angry that anyone would want to harm the dogs. We discussed how it could happen again. I realized I needed to be proactive. I gathered research on animal abuse from *The Link* and *Animal Legal Defense Fund*. I created an incident report to fill out for anyone observed mistreating the dogs. Fortunately, after word got around campus that any mistreatment would not be tolerated, all mistreatment—verbal or throwing things at dogs—stopped. The students started learning that dogs, like people, don't like being teased with no safe place to go.

One student wrote the following, which he read over the PA system along with the morning announcements in the school:

> *Due to my reading of The Tangled Web of Animal Abuse, I've learned a lot from reading about these men being mistreated when they were growing up. They had no respect for women and pets. They became mass murderers due to their childhood. When you hit dogs, it makes them mean and aggressive, just like me.*

Another student wrote (verbatim),

Ms. Dalton I'm having a problem saying sorry. I told you that I loved dogs. I love dogs. When I was little, I had pets. My first and most favorite pet was a dog. I was not trying to be mean to the Dog. I was just throwing the Rock and it hit the cage. I'm really wanting to do something to earn your trust. Well, I'm sorry I maid a mistake. I hope you'll except my apology. Because I really love dogs.

Another issue arose over resentment toward Anthony, Vernon, and Eduardo. They felt they had something good going on and thought they would be respected for their work with the dogs. Some students resented that Anthony, Vernon, and Eduardo had extra privileges and let them know how they felt.

Anthony, Vernon, and Eduardo had grown up around dogs and knew they felt good about themselves when they had a dog to hang out with—even in a correctional facility. However, Anthony, Vernon, and Eduardo didn't let the naysayers get to them. Together with me, they began building the program. We ignored the people who didn't like the idea of dogs in school or complained that the dog handlers were getting special privileges by being in the POOCH program.

SUPERINTENDENT JESTER'S DIRECTIVE

In November 1994, Oregon voters passed Measure 11, establishing mandatory minimum sentencing for several crimes. The measure stipulated that all defendants over age fifteen charged with certain crimes would be tried as adults. The *Oregonian*'s Tony Green wrote, "Proponents of the measure argued that judges had been too lenient in sentencing violent offenders. However, critics often state that Measure 11 is misused by district attorneys. It was stated that prosecutors supported a proposal in the 1995 Legislature to give judges some discretion in second-degree rape cases, but opponents of Measure 11 blocked it because improving the law would make it more difficult to persuade voters to overturn it."

Measure 11 requires youth aged fifteen to seventeen years of age be tried as adults in criminal court when they have been charged with certain listed crimes. If convicted, the youth may be placed in the physical custody of the Oregon Youth Authority until age twenty-five under most conditions. Still, they remain in the legal custody of the Oregon Department of Corrections

(DOC). The mandatory minimum sentences of ten years or more include murder, 25 years; attempt or conspiracy to commit aggravated murder, ten years; attempt or conspiracy to commit murder, seven years, six months; manslaughter in the first degree, ten years.

Little did I know that the superintendent would direct me to change the location of the dog kennels on campus. Since the new sentencing guidelines meant building more housing for the increased population, our first location for the dogs had to be moved. We had already spent the initial $10,000 donation on the kennels and storage area next to the high school. I didn't want the dogs to be isolated from the main campus.

Four tents like the ones used in Desert Storm would be erected in the field where the boys were training their dogs. The POOCH dog structure had to move because barking dogs would keep the boys awake at night when they should have been able to get a good night's sleep.

I assured Jean Vollum, the donor, that we could recycle the metal roofing and fencing in the new location at the far end of campus. But where would we put the dogs while waiting for the new kennel to be completed? We could not leave them where they were because the four tents for the students would soon be erected nearby.

Inside the door to the building trades classes, a large empty classroom temporarily housed the dogs. Thanks to Freddie Mitchell, the building trades instructor, the students put up temporary dog runs with metal

The original kennel by the school had to be moved to a temporary space. (Photo from author's collection.)

framing. Working as a team and learning to assemble metal panels became enjoyable for the students. One of the students said, "This is like the times I had to move from one foster home to the next."

Since the dogs were stuck in the classroom overnight, they had no place other than their designated area to go to the bathroom. When the building trades students entered the building in the morning, they complained loudly about the smell. We had increased the number of dogs in the program, which added to the clean-up time.

I wouldn't say I liked having to house dogs in the area without outdoor access, but it was temporary. I was not pleased that we would have to move to the far end of campus, where students could not see the dogs as they passed from the main school building to classes in the building trades area.

With the location move, the horticulture students got involved in testing the soil for possible pesticides and toxins. They felt their contribution to the program gave them important tasks to complete. Another student researched the best tree in the new area so the dogs could hang out under a tree again.

I began to think of ways to involve more students and dogs. It was clear to me that this would benefit the boys and dogs we rescued and the MacLaren community. When the boys were not working with their dogs or helping build the kennels, I enriched the curriculum by bringing in speakers. On one occasion, the sheriff's department brought a canine to show what he had learned. The dog, imported from Germany, knew German rather than English commands. A boy raised his hand and asked, "Can you teach us the commands?" The sheriff responded, "I am the only one who knows the words."

Dog learning the "sit" command. (Photo from author's collection.)

We also had a staff member show the dog handlers how specially trained dogs can become certified for search and rescue. He would have a youth hide behind a tree and send his dog to search. The youths were fascinated with what dogs can be taught to do. The dog handlers liked showing that their dogs would sit on command. The search and rescue dog trainer often shared how to teach a dog to learn commands other than the basic ones.

The new area for the dog kennel was a large, fenced area where tractors and maintenance equipment had been stored. The shed was falling, but it provided an opportunity to involve the boys in learning new skills, such as building a larger kennel.

Once the enlarged kennel space had been completed, we hosted another grand opening in which we honored guests, donors, and a few MacLaren staff. Of course, refreshments were served with the help of the boys. I warned them, "Stay away from the cookies until the guests have been served first."

We could now add more boys and more dogs. Many students applied to work with school dogs for high school credits. They were allowed to stay in the program until they earned credits in communications, careers, work experience, and some dog DNA science. Once they had earned the credits, they left POOCH to return to the school and earn other needed credits.

One of the boys mentioned that being with others and the dogs was like having a family that cared. Late in the afternoon, after the dogs had been fed and the lights turned out for the night, the dog handlers went to the gate to leave as a group. The supervisor did a count and found one dog handler missing. The supervisor went back inside and turned the lights on, and he found the boy and his dog sitting with each other in the kennel sleeping area. It reminded me of a child wanting his stuffed toy so he could sleep better at night.

On another occasion, we were going to adopt out a dog named Cleo. I couldn't find the dog or the boy. I needed to get the dog loaded in my SUV for a home visit with the adopter. When I walked out of the main building looking for the boy, I found him near the gate with his hoodie pulled over part of his face. He was holding his dog, Cleo. As I got closer, I realized he was crying. He had bonded with his dog, and now I was breaking the bond. The boy's staff was notified that Cleo had been adopted and after-hours counseling may be needed.

Sad youth waiting for his dog to be transported to an adoptive home. His hoodie covers his head as he buries his face in his dog's fur. (Photo from author's collection.)

Dogs provide unconditional love that so many are starving to experience. This observation prompted me to expand dog and boy interactions to a living unit—another good idea from the boys. Later in the program, with approval from the living unit staff, a dog was allowed to spend the night in the living unit. The boy assigned to the dog controlled his dog while in the living unit. It also became an opportunity for those not in the program to experience joy and acceptance from a dog—even if it was just for the night. It brought me joy to see staff witness the value of Project POOCH and how bonding with a dog could help students advance while in their treatment programs in the living unit.

Sometimes, I used a "helper" dog for a new participant in the program. The helper dog assisted with building confidence. For example, Sasha knew the basics and did what was asked of her on the first try. She was a German shepherd mix whose family had turned her into a humane society. She sat in her kennel at the shelter, her back turned to potential adopters. Catherine chose Sasha as a dog for the program. The boys learned humane dog training through positive reinforcement; patience was the most difficult for most boys to learn. Sasha helped boys learn the importance of patience in training dogs.

The boys all smiled when the POOCH van pulled up and Sasha was released to the kennel yard. They wanted to know about her history, which Catherine read from the humane society paperwork.

Sasha liked walking around campus; however, she got loose from her handler when she saw a squirrel running across campus to get to an old, deserted steam tunnel. I looked out an office window and saw Sasha had chased a squirrel to the edge of the campus boundary line. I grabbed an extra leash and some dog treats to catch her. I brought her back and handed the leash to the boy responsible for Sasha. The boys found the entire episode exciting to talk about since the campus perimeter had yet to be fenced. Sasha's handler came to me at the end of the school day to apologize for letting her get loose and asked if it would be hard to find her a home since she seemed to have a strong prey drive for small, furry creatures. I answered that it could be hard for an adopter to control Sasha if she saw a squirrel or a cat. I soon saw the boys getting discouraged because they had trained Sasha, but no one was applying for her.

Sasha continued to be an excellent dog for any new boy because she was so well-trained in her basic commands. I often kept her in my office if her handler had to go to the clinic or elsewhere on campus. She loved sitting in a chair or climbing on my table to look out the window and watch students moving around campus. After a time, Sasha became protective of the office and would bark if someone knocked on my door. I would usually step outside, but that wasn't very practical if someone needed to sit down or have a confidential conversation.

Sasha, a German shepherd mix, patiently sat in my office looking out the window. (Photo from author's collection.)

I soon learned that Sasha and I were bonding, so I decided to take her home for the weekend. She relaxed and gave me a look that communicated: *Thank you for giving me a home.* I now had a dog who would be allowed inside to be part of my family. I paid the fee on Monday morning and completed the application to adopt Sasha. She still came to spend the day helping a boy in the program struggling with his first untrained dog.

Along with the boys, I learned how to solve unexpected problems, which helped improve the program. When I had Saturday morning chats with them, we often became a team of problem solvers. Everyone had an opportunity to be heard and ask questions. This was a new experience for most of them. Sometimes, we can't solve a problem right away, so we agreed to "Sleep on it" and come back the next day to continue our problem-solving.

7

Adding More Boys and More Dogs

1994–1995

The selection process involved applying to participate in the program and getting approval from the living unit treatment manager.

"Do I have to answer questions like a real interview?" asked David.

I replied, "Yes, the more practice you get while locked up, the easier it will be when you get out for job interviews."

The school year from September 1994 to August 1995 enrolled twenty-two students. I wanted a cross section of students from diverse cultures in hopes that dogs would bring everyone together for a common purpose—getting unwanted dogs trained and adopted. Of the twenty-two students, five were Black, ten were white, and seven were Latino.

We selected most of the dogs from the Oregon Humane Society. Yet I had a tough time saying no occasionally when approached by others seeking placement for a dog.

During 1994, we took in Snake, an Australian cattle dog mix, from a relative of one of our major donors; Shadow, a Labrador mix, from a family near campus; Freckles, a poodle mix, from the school tutor; Goldie, a Labrador mix, rescued by a local person who found the dog in a bag on the side of the road; Gretta, a rottweiler mix, from the local veterinarian as a stray; CJ, a Labrador mix, a runaway dog that appeared on campus; and Tux, a German shorthair, from a MacLaren staff member who found the dog as a stray. Additionally, dogs rescued from the Oregon Humane Society included Reno, a Labrador mix; Coco, a golden retriever mix; Yukon, an Australian shepherd mix; Bandit, a German shepherd and Australian cattle dog mix; Sasha, a German shepherd mix; Bear, a corgi mix; Jack, a Labrador retriever; Jordan, a Labrador mix; and Copper, an Australian shepherd and spaniel mix.

When people began contacting me to take their dogs, I realized it was not the right message for the students. My goal was for the students to save abandoned dogs in shelters that could be euthanized due to behavioral problems. I also wanted the students to realize that bringing a dog into a home is a decision that must be carefully made.

Getting our dogs from shelters also saved money on our veterinary expenses. Dogs would be neutered/spayed, receive vaccinations, and so forth. We were fortunate to find a sponsor in the Woodburn Veterinary Clinic. They were very generous in helping with veterinary expenses, and a few years later, Debbie Unrau, DVM, started coming to the kennel once a month to check out the dogs and demonstrate how to handle a dog during an exam.

There was never a boring day at Project POOCH. Students learned kennel management skills, trained dogs, and cared for them. They also learned how to meet and converse with adopters and volunteers.

Due to the unfenced correctional facility, I soon experienced an emergency alert with directions to keep all students at their present location. There was to be no student movement for security reasons. Some students were on the run. Unfortunately, one of the runners was a youth from the program. He was sent to the lockup area at the far end of campus and dismissed from the program. It was an opportunity to let the youth know that such behavior was unacceptable and that there would not be a second chance to return to POOCH.

MacLaren School for Boys is situated off the main freeway between Portland and Salem. The students had headed south on Highway 99, which parallels the freeway. They encountered many side roads to hide from passing automobiles. On one side of the facility lives local farmers, and on the other side is a mobile home park.

The escapees had removed their denim jackets and dropped them off before leaving campus. Their grade slips were in the jacket pockets, so figuring out which boys were on the run was not difficult. About forty-five minutes after the escape, the boys were found at the Last Chance Saloon; no doubt, a sign indicating twenty-four-hour exotic dancers led them there. After every living unit counted the number of boys it had, there was no movement on campus until security verified the head counts.

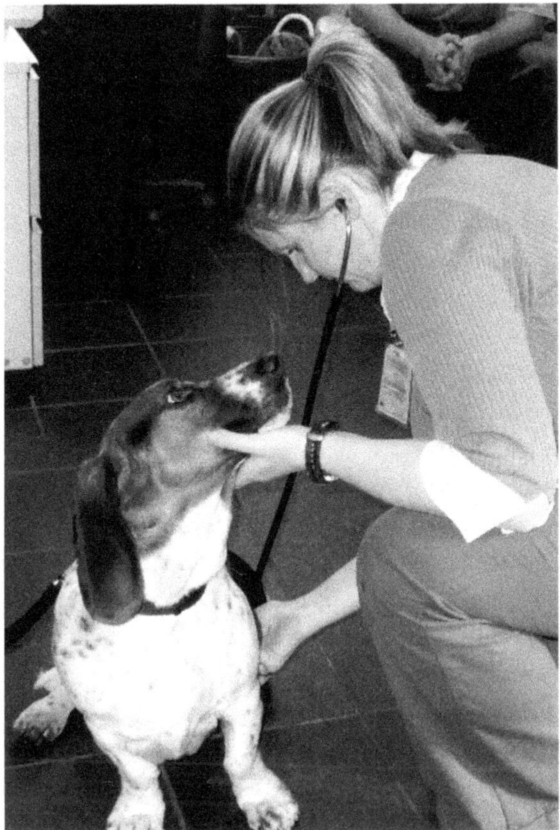

Dr. Debbie Unrau checks the heart of Raskel, the basset hound. (Photo from author's collection.)

BOYS SHOW THEIR CREATIVITY

The boys were producing creative ideas to enhance the program. They suggested that dogs be allowed to go to the gym to acclimate to a lot of human and ball movement while shooting hoops. "We promise to clean up any messes made by the dogs," they said with a smile. We lost the privilege of bringing the dogs to the gym much later because it was to be turned into a visiting center. I was disappointed because I planned to introduce dogs to dock diving since the swimming pool was part of the gym and would also be covered.

It seemed that POOCH grew in unexpected ways every week. The suggestions made by program participants and others enhanced the program for both dogs and boys. There is something very gratifying about getting suggestions and involvement from the boys. They began investing in the program's success. Their ideas were very creative and fun to try with some dog competitions.

Catherine often came up with new things to teach dogs. However, some teachers complained when six chairs were set up in the main hallway about five feet apart so the dogs could learn to weave around chairs.

Dogs begging for food at the human table is quite common. I ordered box lunches so the boys and dogs could practice good manners at the library tables. I said to the dog handlers, "What you reward repeats itself. Once a dog starts getting rewarded for begging at the table, it is difficult to change the behavior."

More boys wanted to participate in the program when they saw the dogs walking around campus or playing in a huge nearby field.

Since MacLaren is halfway between Portland and Salem, I decided to try searching for dogs at the Willamette Humane Society in Salem. I started videotaping available dogs and took the videos back to the boys for their input in selecting dogs for Project POOCH.

BOYS HELP SELECT DOGS

Every dog enclosure had a card, called a cage card, on the front, giving information about the dog. Videotaping the cards helped the boys develop their decision-making skills. After the boys had made their selections, I returned to the humane society to assess the dogs' temperament, a requirement of MacLaren. Dr. Emily Weiss developed the widely used 'Meet Your Match" test, and the boys had fun learning how to use the color-coded program to evaluate their dogs and the people looking to adopt them to match their personalities, energy levels, and needs. The boys practiced using the test on the dogs in the program to see how they had progressed. It was interesting to allow them to "grade" their dogs. Testing includes dog stare, sensitivity, tag, pinch, food aggression, rawhide aggression, and dog-to-dog aggression. The dog is given a grade from A to F for each part of the test. We could not bring in a dog with a bite history or severe aggressiveness. We wanted dogs with behavioral problems, such as jumping on people, so the boys could extinguish the unruly behavior. There were always many larger homeless dogs needing to be rescued.

I went to the shelter and found a Labrador with a calm temperament. He was getting passed over because he was plain-looking and weighed sixty-five pounds. After evaluating him, I loaded him in my SUV and surprised Eduardo when he arrived at the kennel after lunch in his living unit. Eduardo liked the name Jack. Jack had been with us for a brief time when he appeared lame. Catherine took him to the veterinary clinic, and Jack was diagnosed with a bad case of hip dysplasia, a hereditary genetic disease that, if left untreated, eventually leads to death. Since the needed surgery would cost more than the program had in reserve, we gathered donations by letting donors know about Jack's need through direct contact and our newsletter.

EDUARDO OBSERVES HIS DOG'S SURGERY

Catherine arranged for an orthopedic surgeon to do surgery at Slocum's Veterinary Clinic. With proper supervision, Eduardo was allowed to go with Jack to the clinic and observe the surgery. Nikki DeBuse, of the *Woodburn Independent*, wrote, "Staff collected more than $2,000 in private donations to pay for two surgeries that repaired Jack's hip sockets. The dysplasia, which staff discovered only after bringing Jack to MacLaren, was so severe that the dog's hips actually popped out of the sockets, causing Jack great pain."

Eduardo had to put on a sterile gown and cap to witness the surgeon placing the wedges in Jack's bone. Jack stayed at the clinic all night so he could be observed. Eduardo could not stop talking about his unexpected experience watching Jack's surgery. He told the other youth in the program that he was worried and scared as he watched the surgery in the glassed-in theater at the clinic. He said, "I felt like a real veterinarian."

Jack couldn't walk for weeks following his operation. The youth borrowed a food cart from the campus kitchen, and they rolled Jack along with the other dogs during walks. They were proud of their creativity, and they kept Jack on a strict rehab program. The dog was adopted by a construction worker who spotted Jack while erecting the four tents due to the passage of Measure 11.

Boys still had the responsibility to write in their journals daily. I read them to see if anything needed to be addressed. Many males are taught not to show their feelings—especially in front of their peers. Reading their journals was a way for me to address a boy's struggles with his dog or staff. A few of the journal entries:

12/93—My first day went just great except for the dog I worked with is a little stubborn. But it will take a while for the dog to get used to me. Anyway, my counselor doesn't like the fact that I'm working with the dog. If I could talk to you before school is out it would help me with my counselor. [I wrote the following response: "One way to deal with your counselor is to let him know how much you appreciate that he is letting you work with the dogs."]

12/94—Goldie was extremely hyper today. Learning slowly with me but still wants to do his own thing. Practicing patience while cleaning Goldie's pen. He's been very loud while waiting for me. He was restless today. I'm becoming attached, I think.

Early in the program, I would bring in a dog and say to a particular boy, "This is your dog to care for and train." I soon discovered the boys were developing a strong bond with "their dog," and they were often upset when the dog was adopted.

I later changed my approach and said, "This is the program's dog. It is your job to get him/her ready for a home." I shared letters from adopters describing how well their adopted dog was trained, and some adopters brought their dogs back for additional training to let the youth see how happy the dog was in a new home. A few possible job openings were also offered to the young men when they were released from corrections. I was happy to see boys responding to new learning opportunities—especially when supportive veterinarians enriched the program by giving vaccinations, microchipping, and bringing samples of various parasites found on and in dogs. We also discussed how what they learn about humanely treating dogs and correcting behaviors works with children. The boys were now dog parents.

MAJOR INCIDENT OCCURS

It had been a busy day, and I was ready to leave when I received a call from our major donor, Jean Vollum. She and her family would be taking an extended trip to many countries, and she asked, "Can I board my dog Snake at the kennel while we are on our trip?"

We had never considered boarding dogs other than ours; however, I quickly agreed to board Snake.

Since Jack's ability to go on walks was limited due to his hip dysplasia surgery, Eduardo said he could help with Snake. Snake weighed thirty pounds and was chestnut brown.

I was still trying to avoid working on weekends so I could do other things; however, that changed with a phone call late one Sunday.

"The dogs escaped?" I repeated. Bob reported he had left Anthony and Vernon to take care of Grover and Snake while he went to supervise recreation in SITP. According to Anthony, he had said to Vernon, "I hope they don't run." Well, that is exactly what happened.

My heart sank. There was no time to waste. It was the time of year when the sun went down early, and it would soon be dark. I pulled on my boots and grabbed a coat, leashes, and a bag of dog treats. I started driving around Woodburn, hoping to see the dogs; however, they had been missing for several hours. I drove on the side roads as I called for them. It was getting dark, and I had to suspend my search until the next day. Eduardo made lost dog signs. I contacted the local Spanish-speaking radio station, which aired information about our missing dogs. I tried anything that was suggested to bring them back. The popular advice was that they would get hungry and find their way back, but I couldn't wait for that to happen. This was an emergency.

Someone suggested I get a large sausage, tie a rope on one end, and drive around with it hanging out my car window. I did so, looking in my rearview mirror and hoping to see two dogs running after the car with the sausage hanging out the window. I wanted to return to campus with good news but was discouraged.

I called Harry Oakes, the owner of a K-9 search and rescue organization, for help. He involved the boys by having them collect any dog hair from Grover's bed in the kennel. Harry's dog took in the smell from the collected hair, and his dog went searching. Harry could only say that the scent wore off at the Pudding River.

After seeing a lost dog sign, a woman called, saying she had a black dog that could be Grover. Immediately, I took off to see if it was. It was a black dog, about fifty-five pounds, with a wire around his neck. It wasn't Grover.

A month after the escape, a corrections staff member walked outside the facility grounds and found a deceased dog matching Grover's description in a ditch near a wide shoulder of the road. I went right away and found it to be Grover. His collar and tag were on, and his body was intact—no cuts, no physical trauma, no marks on him to indicate he was hit by a truck or automobile. Oregon law states that farmers can kill a dog harassing any livestock. I believe Grover was poisoned and dumped near campus because his tag identified him with the address of the correctional facility. I took Grover to be cremated. The ashes are still with me. I plan to scatter them in an area outside the fenced area of MacLaren.

Not long after Grover was found, the man who ran the boarding kennel a mile north of MacLaren found Snake in a ditch. I picked up his body and took it to the Woodburn Veterinary Clinic for a necropsy. The veterinarian told me the dog had been dead too long to know what had caused Snake's death. Like Grover, he had no marks on him, and his collar and tag remained around his neck.

My voice cracked when I told the boys their beloved dogs were gone. Anthony and Vernon were heartbroken. Anthony was upset that he had laughingly commented to Vernon about hoping the dogs wouldn't run. Snake had become Eduardo's favorite dog. On February 4, he wrote,

> *Well the day went good until I found out that Snake died. It hit me hard. So hard that I was confused with my emotions that I didn't know which emotion was which. But I will always remember the good times that I had with him. He make me feel like I was someone important. I remember when I first saw him barking up a storm like he was going to eat me, so I sat by the gate until he stopped barking. Then I opened the gate and I new that I had a friendship that would never end. Even though he is gone our friendship is still there. He was the kind of dog that I was proud of having. Snake was the one that kept me in first place in training. He never let me down. He never made me mad at him. Maybe frustrated but never mad. I loved him. I will never forget him. He was my one true friend. One that will always be with me. I will never forget the way he made me feel good all over. Snake you will always be with me in my heart. I will never forget you and the way you made me feel. Snake you are a true pal—one that will stay in my heart and mind.*

Snake if you can hear me, I love you and I will never forget you. I hope you understand that I will always love you. Bye Pal. I love you and I will miss you. Bye, bye. Stay free. You will always be number 1. Be free.

Eduardo asked if he could have Snake's ashes placed in a nearby river the way Native Americans often did. "I want to send him back to the creator," he said.

Jean Vollum was gracious and realized how difficult it was for POOCH to record this incident. She agreed to let Eduardo have Snake's ashes.

We added more safety measures to our list of priorities.

8

Dogs Saving Humans

1995–1996

I soon learned there was no typical day at Project POOCH because there were so many moving parts. Each day was unique, with new dogs and boys joining the program to earn high school credits, new trainers giving lessons, potential adopters meeting dogs, film crews, volunteers, speakers, and unexpected issues. The program wasn't just about boys saving dogs; the dogs were also saving the boys and the adopters.

The boys were learning that they were saving dogs that had been abandoned, much like them. Boys and dogs are often in many placements before coming to MacLaren School for Boys, the strictest incarceration facility in Oregon. Glen, a fifteen-year-old, was abandoned by his mother when he was a toddler. He'd been in forty placements and several abusive foster care homes before coming to MacLaren.

While reading the history of the dog he had been working with, he said, "Annie was in a home until she was no longer a puppy. Her family put her on Craigslist. Then, she was in the humane society before being sent to a foster home. Now she's here with me." He stared at Annie's history and said, "She was never wanted—just like me." He started talking to Annie and told her how much he respected her and how he would care for her. Then he mentioned that everyone deserves respect.

The boys became empowered when their dogs learned the basic commands through mutual respect. Many of the incarcerated boys struggled emotionally due to their past abuse, and, sometimes for the first time, they experienced unconditional love from the dogs in their care.

LETTING GO OF THE PAST

When Max was incarcerated at MacLaren, his parents came to see him twice. They then left Oregon for a new life and erased his birthday from their minds. When Max was interviewed to be accepted into the program, he shared his love for dogs. At age twelve, he had a boxer he could hardly wait to see when he came home from school each day. One day, he got home and called his dog, but the animal never came. He thought it was strange because his dog always met him. He asked his dad if he knew where his dog was, and his father told him the landlord said they had to get rid of the dog or he would kick the family out of the apartment. I listened as he told me, "I bawled over my dog and took off to my grandma's house. I never asked about my dog again. It was just too painful."

Every boy often has a favorite dog. Max's favorite was a dog in the program named Dale. Dale was a one-and-a-half-year-old when he came to POOCH with the name Hero. The shelter had listed him as a shorthair Labrador mix—a hunting dog. Max changed his name to Dale after his hero, the race car driver Dale Earnhardt. Max looked through dog books and decided to change Dale's breed to Great Dane/dairy cow because he was white with large black spots. Dale learned basic obedience and some tricks to add to his potential to be adopted.

Max's staff liked the idea when he requested to bring Dale back to the living unit during lunch. Max said, "Boys in my living unit were often jealous because I got to work with the dogs. I had to keep others from giving Dale people food. This taught me how to correct people without getting into a fistfight."

One Saturday morning, I was supervising the program due to staff absence. Security soon informed me that I could not pick up one of the dog handlers, Billy, because he needed to see a counselor. The youth's brother had been shot and killed the night before.

I told security the youth would not understand why I would not pick him up to work with the dogs. He was a good dog handler and was part of the POOCH family. As I picked up the other dog handlers, they asked why I wasn't picking up Billy. When I told them what had happened, Max said, "Let's bring my dog Dale to be with Billy."

I rang the buzzer on the living unit. A staff member came and allowed Max to bring Dale inside to be with Billy. Billy started crying as he flung himself on his bed and curled up in a ball. Dale jumped on the bed and started licking Billy's tears. Sometimes, a dog can help the healing process better than a human. We left Dale with Billy for the rest of the day and continued our dog walks and tasks at the kennel. At the end of the day, we went to pick up Dale and put him in his kennel for the night. Billy hugged Dale and said, "Thank you for making me feel better."

DOG LOVE NEVER ENDS

Sometimes, people adopt a dog and give it up because they are moving. That wasn't the case after Boogie was adopted from Project POOCH. The adopter, Meghan, wrote,

> *I was thankful every day for finding my perfect friend and companion. He saw me through a marriage break-up, falling back in love, moving overseas, and having my two babies. I couldn't have had a better partner through it all. Boogie died last week, and even though I am completely gutted, I am thankful for all the days I had with him. He was 12, and I thought (besides some arthritis) he was as healthy as possible. I thought we had a couple of years left. But it turns out he had cancer of the spleen, which had spread to his liver. In the space of nine hours, he went from being completely fine and happy to being gone in his sleep. I wanted to let you know Boogie had a happy and full life and provided me with the same right up to the end. Thank you for helping us find each other.*

Another letter came from Alexis Del Cid, a former Portland television reporter. The letter read,

> *We had just lost our dog, Saint, who had died at 17 years old. It was a heartbreaking loss, and we were so blue.*
>
> *A month later, my husband decided it would be fun to go to a dog show—to people-watch and dogwatch! He knew it would cheer us up. But low and behold, at the dog show, there was a booth run by a special organization I had done a news story on called Project POOCH.*
>
> *I visited the MacLaren Youth Facility to visit Project POOCH, where a select group of boys love, care for, rehabilitate, and train mistreated dogs. Meeting the boys who care for these sweet creatures and learning so much from doing so was powerful. It was one of the most powerful stories I'd ever enjoyed covering. The care they showed the dogs and how they spoke about them were insightful.*

We walked up to the booth and asked if they had any dogs that would be great family dogs. The person at the booth said, we just rescued two boxers. One was already adopted, but we still have the other one.

Ten minutes later, we had an appointment to see the boxer. I had already named him Buster.

My husband and I brought our little boy to meet him. One of the boys brought Buster out on his leash, and he looked so big! Buster made a wiggly b-line for our son, with his ears back and the closest thing to a smile you'll ever see on a dog! He sniffed our son's face and gave his cheek a lick. Our son giggled. They were about the same height. We signed every paper we needed to sign, and when Buster arrived for his overnight test visit, I knew he would never leave. He was ours.

Buster was the truest, most loyal, funny, and loving companion our family could have ever dreamed of. He came with me on every single kid pick-up, errand, walk, hike, jog, road trip, outdoor lunch, and anything else where a dog could go. There wasn't a lap he didn't sit in or a bed he didn't like to snuggle in. He was our cherished family member. Our sweet 75-pound lap dog. We pampered him with love for ten years and gave him treats and Christmas presents. We made up songs about him. We took thousands of pictures of him. He was quite literally the star of our family. I took him to school show-and-tells, soccer games, and football games. Throughout my 25-year news career, Buster was on television with me multiple times in Portland, Oregon, Kansas City, and San Antonio. Whether it was a holiday promo, a news story about something dog-related, or a fundraiser for a big dog walk—if it involved me, Buster was part of it. He also had quite the following on Facebook and Instagram.

He enjoyed canoe rides, boat rides, and paddleboard rides. He went inner tubing with me and swam in rivers and lakes. People would tell me how beautiful he was, and I felt so lucky, marveling that of all the dogs in the universe, we got Buster.

What a gift. Buster was a beautiful soul, and we miss him terribly. We call them rescue dogs because humans have rescued them from terrible conditions, but honestly, I think it's more accurate to say they rescued us. I know that's the case with Buster.

When I think of all the joy and love that came into our lives with him and how much love and joy we can share and bring into his life, I realize that, as humans, we are meant to keep giving and creating love and joy. We're meant to keep giving and receiving that love. And it is possible to do that while missing someone as much as we miss sweet Buster. I like to think that he changed our lives for the better. He was such a gift, and every time I look around at the countless pictures of sweet Buster around our house, I know we're all better for having had him in our lives.

9

Emotions from the Past

1995–1996

Changes due to Measure 11 were soon to be implemented. I completely disagreed with this legislative action but was powerless to change it. Videos were produced to show students in public schools what Measure 11 was and its consequences. Oregon voters overwhelmingly passed Measure 11 in November 1994. Known as Oregon's "one-strike, you're out" law, Measure 11 sets mandatory minimum sentences for certain crimes, bars early release, leave, or reduced sentence, and requires persons aged fifteen to seventeen years of age to be tried as adults in criminal court when they have been charged with certain crimes.

Vernon was allowed to speak to two hundred concerned citizens at a special hearing. The special hearing was held at the King Facility and called by Representative Avel Gordly and State Senator Jeannette Hamby. Vernon was photographed as he spoke to the crowd. He was applauded when he said, "You've got to keep hope alive. All kids are salvageable—lock them away, and they lose hope and life."

I would need to work harder to help our boys. The facility changed its name to MacLaren Youth Correctional Facility. The incarcerated would no longer be referred to as *boys*; they were now *youth offenders*. Measure 11 would also mean an increase in the number of incarcerated youths.

Anthony and Vernon had been released before the enactment of Measure 11.

ABANDONED GRAVESITES

I continued to help on Saturdays due to the ongoing staffing problem. One such Saturday presented a discovery while walking the dogs and youths to the back area where our new kennel would be located. We saw deserted buildings from earlier times where horses and pigs had been housed on a working farm that provided meat and vegetables. We stopped when we saw five gravesites around the base of a huge tree. Curiosity got the better of me, and I wanted to know more about the bodies buried there. Our youths wanted to know more, too. They were sad that the final resting place for the boys buried at the base of the tree was a correctional site. One youth said, "When I get out of here, I'm never coming back. Not even dead."

With research compiled by Stephenie Flora from oregonpioneers.com, Roberta MacLaren provided information about the Oregon State Reform School cemetery that I later shared with the youths.

Frank Dilley—Born in 1893, Died July 6, 1910—Pulmonary tuberculosis.

Benny Jackson—Born in 1891, Died April 15, 1908—Tuberculosis (formerly from Alaska).

John Marshall—No date of birth. Either age thirteen or fifteen. He had recovered from measles when he suffered a relapse; his parents lived in California. His parents gave orders to bury his remains at the school.

Hiram Mcrea—Born in 1891, Died May 5, 1908—Cardia paralysis following diphtheria, formerly from Medford.

No information for the fifth gravesite was found.

I shared the information while we were on a dog walk. The youths did not talk much. Even the dogs sensed the youths' emotions. It was quiet as we thought about the ones who never got out of MacLaren. As I called the youths back to their living units for lunch, I sensed that they were talking with each other about the gravesites.

In about a year, perimeter fencing would be installed, stopping access to the areas with a long-forgotten history of MacLaren School for Boys.

At first, I did not like moving to the far end of campus, but I had an "aha" moment—I could add more dog runs. I wanted to recycle as much as possible. In the meantime, we had to address where to house the dogs.

A NEW AREA FOR THE DOGS

The youth were enjoying their newfound area for the kennel. They now had space with a couch and computers to prepare dog flyers. They could listen to music and learn dog massage, pet first aid, and yoga. And there was a coffee pot, which was my requirement. We were getting a lot of interest internationally. I spoke to and assisted correctional facilities in other countries with the logistics of starting their dog programs. Meeting and collaborating with people from South Korea, Japan, and the United Kingdom also broadened my learning.

Kotomi Kamiyama founded Kidogs in Japan after learning about Project POOCH and then visiting our site to learn more. I also met Tominaga Kayoko while presenting at the fourth annual Live Love Animals International Symposium in Kobe, Japan. It was a cultural learning experience as they told me how they shaped their programs to meet the needs of Japanese youth.

Japanese author Noriko Imanishi visited Project POOCH and wrote about the program and its participants when she came to the United States. A boy in the Nara Youth Correctional Facility in Nara, Japan, had read her book and was impressed. I was invited to copresent with Noriko. The students stood up in unison as we approached the podium. After I spoke, questions were permitted. The question that has really stayed with me is, "What is unconditional love?"

To this day, Noriko and her photographer husband remain dear friends.

Samsung funded a facility in South Korea and asked me to be their consultant. The ribbon cutting brought out uniformed dignitaries and a tour of their state-of-the-art facility for dogs.

Echo Glen detention center in Washington state modeled its program Canine Connections after Project POOCH. The residents are boys ages ten to sixteen and girls ages ten to twenty-one, who have committed serious crimes.

CHANGE HAPPENS

I also realized that our new site was too removed from where students would be during the day. I had no choice if I were to keep the program. It was a large, fenced area where tractors and maintenance equipment were stored. The shed was falling, but what an opportunity to involve the dog handlers in learning new skills, such as building a larger kennel. My vision of more dogs and more students joining the program was much better than staying with just a few dogs and handlers. I began seeing the glass as half full rather than half empty.

A partial building that needs renovation to be a kennel. (Photo from author's collection.)

Two youths measure and prepare the soil so it is flat before the cement is poured. (Photo from author's collection.)

The building trades students were learning real-life framing skills, leveling the soil, installing doors to the dog runs, and pouring and finishing concrete work. They were so proud of themselves when I purchased a tool belt for each worker. I could see the positive attitude when a youth learned a new skill such as using a jackhammer. I liked that the youths were discovering that they didn't always have to ask permission for every action. Such was the case after the cement was poured and still wet, and a youth very

After taking care of their dogs, youths learn how to apply sheetrock to the inside of the building. (Photo from author's collection.)

A supervisor stands near a youth learning how to use a jackhammer to break up concrete. (Photo from author's collection.)

carefully helped his dog make a paw imprint.

When the students were not working with their dogs or helping build the kennels, I enriched the curriculum by bringing in speakers. Education Director of the Oregon Humane Society Carol Shiveley came several times to talk about the proper care of dogs, which included the importance of play and learning time. A prosecutor from the Animal Legal Defense Fund went over Oregon animal laws. The Zimmers and Filsingers brought their art and counseling skills to the dog handlers.

After the youths poured and smoothed the cement for the additional building, they helped a dog do a pawprint. (Photo from author's collection.)

Youth coach from Success Academy, Barbara King, taught social manners and how to meet and greet others. I kept adding speakers as I went along, learning about dog massage, agility, scent work, search and rescue, yoga, and canine basic and advanced certification tests.

One of my fun tasks was to go to a shelter and choose dogs for the program. I wanted a dog that had been overlooked and was at least six months old. It took at least forty-five minutes to test a dog for the program. When I went to one shelter, I asked the kennel manager, "Are there any dogs, in particular, you suggest I look at?" The kennel manager, Cindy, took me to a kennel where a medium-sized dog looked slightly confused. "What is the dog's name?" I asked.

She responded, "Rusty."

A childhood memory surfaced as I recalled my dog named Rusty. I was in the seventh grade when my dad brought another dog home from a man he knew at work. Rusty was very sweet. My dad said, "Rusty wasn't a good city dog and had been kept on a long chain since the people had no fenced yard." We didn't have fencing, so Rusty was again put on a long chain by our house.

On a Saturday, my dad loaded his four older children in his pickup truck, and we headed out to pick blackberries. Our new dog, Rusty, was in the back with me and my siblings. After several hours of berry picking, Dad put the flats of berries into the truck's bed and then signed for Rusty to jump in. Rusty landed right in the middle of the berries.

That upset him, and he started swearing at Rusty. I couldn't help but think how he could have been so dumb as to put the blackberries near the tailgate. Of course, Rusty soon disappeared. We never saw him again. I was so deep in thought that I had not heard Cindy ask me if I wanted to test Rusty for the program. "Oh, yes," I answered. Before I even tested Rusty, I knew this was my second chance. I was excited about signing the paperwork for Rusty to come to Project POOCH and find an adopter to love him and give him a forever home.

Rusty took to training but let it be known that he didn't care much for other dogs.

"When we do his flyer, we must say that Rusty must be the only dog," I told the dog handlers. "We must tell adopters everything we know about a particular dog."

It took a while for Rusty to find a forever home, but he did. I placed him with a young couple in a new apartment in Portland. There was a dog wash station since we get a lot of rain, which means muddy paws. Before leaving Rusty in his new home, I told the adopters, "Before you get in the elevator, make sure there are no other dogs inside." We have since heard from the couple about how great Rusty is doing in his home.

A part of me finally felt some peace over my dog Rusty and the memories from my childhood. I was able to save another Rusty.

10

Expanding School Offerings

1995–1996

The boys and the dogs were thriving. Boys earned high school credits to graduate, and dogs found homes. Adopters openly expressed how well-trained their dogs were and how happy the family was with their new family member.

In September 1995, I prepared to share the Project POOCH program at the 7th International Conference on Human-Animal Interactions in Geneva, Switzerland. This exposure was the springboard for much discussion and planning for programs in correctional facilities in Europe and Asia.

I prepared a handout so conference participants could better understand the backgrounds of those boys selected to be part of the POOCH program, the kinds of treatment required while in corrections, where we acquired our dogs, the application to be accepted into the program, MacLaren School fact sheet, various charts indicating ages and races, and an article I had written, "What Animals Teach Us," published in 1991 in *Our Animal WARDS*. In two years, the program had overcome many hurdles, including dealing with grief when dogs died unexpectedly. I didn't shy away from the challenges and disappointments. (See appendix for the handout.)

After spending four days sharing and learning from others at the conference, I returned to the United States motivated and excited about what I had learned.

In talking with Superintendent Robert Jester and others at the facility, I learned that a support system was the weakest link when the young men were released from MacLaren. Many could not go back to their families. They needed a place to live and work.

Released youth found that applying for a job required an online application. Finding their way around downtown Portland was sometimes difficult because of new buildings, and finding the bus transit center could be frustrating.

SUPPORTING TEACHERS

I began asking employers about what they were looking for in an employee and why an employee would be fired. I gathered the information and built a curriculum and speakers around the world of work. It was not unusual for the youths to have never applied for or held a job.

Although I loved seeing the progress made by the student dog handlers in the program, I sensed I needed to pay more attention to the administrative part of my job, which was working with teachers. One day, I was in shock and disbelief when I walked into the staff lounge, and one of the teachers said, "This is our lounge, and you aren't allowed in here." I was astounded and returned to my small office. The previous administrator had a loose leadership/accountability style, and the teachers liked it. One teacher liked responding to some of my questions by saying, "Status quo."

The vocational teachers came from the trades and could be hired as teachers without an education degree. They often had the most difficulty handling the students in their classes. The students liked the "hands-on" approach to learning; however, no one wanted to deal with an angry student with a tool in his hand that could be used to hit another person.

Due to their skills, the special education teachers generally had better outcomes with problem students. This gave me an idea that would hopefully improve teaching skills and learning outcomes.

Cooperative learning was extremely popular around this time. What if I paired a special education teacher with a regular teacher so that they could learn from each other? There was no risk in trying. After my plan was in place and I had solicited input from some of the teachers, I gave it a week before I decided to ask for feedback. The weakness was that one teacher would sit at a computer and do work while the other dealt with the students. The plan was not successful.

However, one teacher introduced the idea of having live rats in her classroom. Most of the students liked the idea. If they completed their assignments successfully, they could play with the rats. I saw one student laughing as he let a rat climb over him.

Another teacher allowed a student to bring a yellow Labrador retriever he had named Nike into the classroom while he worked on a computer. He brought a bone for Nike to chew on during class.

The teacher came over to remove the bone, and the student said, "No, don't do that. Nike doesn't like anyone to take his bone." The teacher continued toward Nike, saying, "All dogs like me," as she reached for the bone. Nike bit her, which resulted in dogs no longer being allowed in classrooms.

PLANNING SIGNIFICANT EVENTS

Tying significant events with book learning was needed. I started with a presentation in the auditorium to celebrate Black History Month, followed a few months later by Cinco de Mayo. These events encouraged the students to participate. We often had legislators and administrators from the central office join in and watch the performances.

We had invited Bobby, a Black dancer, to teach the students how to tie-dye and wear their completed work as they performed an African dance. Many refused to learn how to dance. I talked with Bobby about it, and we compromised by shortening the time the students would dance and using fewer dancers. An incentive was built into the compromise. The students could go to an unused building with a kitchen to prepare and eat soul food.

For Cinco de Mayo, we had piñatas for the POOCH dog handlers outside near the kennel so the dogs could watch something interesting and fun. The main event was in the auditorium for the entire campus. I had invited some professional flamenco dancers and a professor from a local community college to present a historical slide show on Latinos in Oregon.

All the students were seated in the auditorium by their living unit, and there was a special section for visitors, such as legislators and community leaders. Students from SITP were relegated to a special section and closely supervised.

The history presentation was to be first, and the dancers were last. I was keeping track of time and began to worry when the history presentation didn't seem to be getting close to its end.

The dancers were backstage and ready to perform; however, I told them it would be a little longer since the other presentation had not ended. They were not pleased. Now, I was anxious.

I went to the history professor and said, "You must end your presentation because the dancers need to go on." He just kept talking and showing slides.

I headed backstage again to tell the dancers to please be patient. They felt they had been patient enough and threatened to walk out if they could not go on immediately. I then went to the side of the stage and had the curtain pulled while the history professor was still presenting his slides with commentary. The dancers came on with much applause from the audience. That was the end of the event.

A longtime staff member hired to work specifically with Native Americans to maintain their cultural ties while locked up put on an annual event—native dancers wearing their regalia performed. Small groups of students rotated and stopped at stations where they could learn about basket weaving and native foods. Fry bread was extremely popular with the students because they got to sample it.

Meanwhile, I kept adding new classes in the school, such as computer and careers classes. Of course, this meant hiring more teachers.

The saddest interview I ever conducted involved a young woman dressed in blue jeans and a T-shirt. When I asked her why she wanted the job, her response was not what I had expected. She said, "I live in felony flats in Portland and want to get my children out."

Some teachers did not like the new classes I implemented—guitars, dogs, and parenting all involved noise.

Sometimes, working with the dog handlers and the dogs was more enjoyable.

I sought out teachers with dogs to help me build a bridge between the Project POOCH program and traditional high school classes. The science teacher allowed a husky and a rottweiler to visit his class so he could teach the students about genetics. The guitar teacher invited POOCH youth to stand in the hallway while the students played "Hang Down Your Head Tom Dooley" on their guitars. A reading teacher allowed a student to bring his dog to class and sit quietly during the lesson.

I continued sharing Project POOCH's success at conferences and expanded my knowledge about human-animal bond research and other programs. While in the audience at one of the conferences, I sat next to Dr. Lynette Hart from the University of California, Davis.

RECEIVING GOOD ADVICE

When I auspiciously sat next to her, Dr. Hart said, "Anecdotes about your program are great; however, it is important to have qualitative research as well." That ended up being a gem of advice. The problem I saw was how to pay for someone to do the research.

Less than a year later, I received a request from a doctoral student, Sandra Merriam, of Pepperdine University, requesting to use Project POOCH as a research project for her doctoral dissertation. She came to Oregon and spent time conducting interviews with POOCH youth and living unit treatment managers. Her study concluded that Project POOCH works. Human-animal interaction provides the catalyst to allow an extremely troubled youth to view life in a new way. She wrote, "Participants after POOCH indicate positive behavioral characteristics. The general overview is that the program has made dramatic changes in attitude."

Kate Grace Davis, MSW, presented research at the National Technology Assessment Workshop on Animal Assisted Interventions for Youth at Risk in Baltimore, Maryland. Her research had been conducted while affiliated with Portland State University's Graduate School of Social Work. Her publication, "Perspectives of Youth in an Animal-Centered Correctional Vocational Program: A Qualitative Evaluation of Project POOCH," provides insight into the experiences of the fourteen youth who participated in the study. In this evaluation, participating youth described developing patience, experiencing an emotional connection with dogs in the program, and developing practical employment skills, including improved communication with staff, peers, and people from outside the community.

Kristi Racer, of OYA Research and Evaluation, conducted "Research Update: Project POOCH, July 2018." Of the 135 male youth participants, 90 percent were serving Department of Corrections sentences. Fifty percent were Caucasian, 28 percent were Hispanic, 15 percent were African American, and 7 percent were of unknown origin. The average age range was fifteen to twenty-four, and 83 percent of those released to the community had no new felony convictions within three years.

11

Contagious Energy

1995–1996

There was a definite difference in the attitudes of those in POOCH and some of those attending classes in the campus high school. Those in POOCH took on their dogs' energy and weren't shy about showing their feelings. Those in the high school were to be quiet and to move in an orderly fashion when they changed classrooms—no talking or touching others.

The dogs became the conduit for relaxation and fun, along with the work assigned at the kennel. Dogs were learning how to turn out lights. A student named Don trained his dog to stand on her back legs and put her front legs on the handle of a lawn mower like she was mowing grass. Everyone was more relaxed when learning was fun.

The students also pranked me from time to time. One Saturday, I walked into the classroom and saw this big spider climbing down the wall. Of course, I yelled, and they thought my response was hilarious. A youth was in the attic opening and had discretely slid the fake spider down the wall.

When Dr. Debbie Unrah brought roundworms in a jar, the youths thought it was cool to see something so gross. Learning how to hold a dog when getting vaccinations and other skills empowered the dog handlers. The standards were high, but they thrived on positive reinforcement like the dogs they trained. Getting into POOCH meant more freedom to walk around campus, which was a desired goal. From time to time, someone would say how good it felt to be away from their living unit and the issues of others.

DOGS HELPED DAKOTA

Dakota's story is an example of how dogs changed him. He said, "I wasn't sure what MacLaren was when I first got sent here. I thought it was some camp or something. I was in a unit for drug and alcohol treatment."

A youth he met in treatment told him about Project POOCH, and he noted, "I always loved dogs—no matter where I lived, there had always been a dog. I knew I had to get into this program. I didn't trust anyone I met at MacLaren. Everybody would turn on you in a heartbeat. But a dog? I'd be able to trust a dog, and I was desperate for a friend to spend even a little time with, someone I loved and who loved me back."

Dakota was nervous when he heard that his application had passed the first round and that he would be interviewed: "It wasn't just Ms. Dalton I had to talk to. All the kids in the program would be there, too. I knew I had to have one of the best two scores to get in since they only had two openings."

He was thrilled to learn he'd been accepted. He said, "I felt that, finally, something had gone my way. I was going to have a best friend. I wouldn't be so alone. And I thought how great it would be to help train a dog so he could get out. I saw the dogs as criminals like me. They were locked up, too. Somebody had said they were no good. Nobody wanted them. And if I could train them and help them behave, they'd be free."

Dakota also knew the program would keep him busy, and he desperately wanted to fill his time with something besides obsessing about how much time he still had left to serve. He noted that when he started in the program, "POOCH had been around for a while. There were five kennels toward the back of campus. I helped build fences, which was a good feeling. I liked doing something useful and felt good that I was contributing to something that would help dogs. Working with the other kids was a new experience, too. Instead of feeling like someone might turn on me, I felt like we were all working for a good cause. Everybody in the program was like me, wanting to make things work out right."

Ezra was his first dog. He said,

> *I shared him with another youth. We both loved that dog and were so excited to have a dog we didn't mind sharing. We'd each take turns training him and then play with him together. The three of us had fun running around, playing games, or relaxing. The other guy and I had different training styles, so we had to learn to talk to each other about what we were doing so Ezra didn't get confused. I learned I wasn't always right and sometimes had to compromise for Ezra's sake. I learned to disagree without punching somebody out because they didn't see things my way.*

Within a couple of months, Ezra was adopted. Dakota noted, "I knew I'd miss him, but seeing him go home with a family who would love him and treat him right was a great feeling. And he would be free. No more lockup."

Freedom meant a lot to Dakota, and working with the dogs allowed him to walk around campus with his dog. He commented,

> *I never paid attention to the perimeter fence when I was with the dogs. I just blanked the fence out and felt like I was in a park, free. That's when I started acting right.*
>
> *They say, fake it until you make it. I started doing that because if I got in trouble, I would be out of POOCH, and I didn't want that to happen. So, I started behaving like I should, staying out of fights, paying attention in treatment programs, talking things through, facing myself, and somehow, I became a better person. I saw what an asshole I'd been when I'd been sent to MacLaren. I didn't want to be that person anymore. I saw a better way to act and wanted to be a better person.*

Mugsly was Dakota's second dog, one he still thinks about constantly: "He was a chocolate Lab. I was never into Labs, but the second Ms. Dalton brought him in, something clicked, and I knew I wanted him. Ms. Dalton was a little hesitant at first because I hadn't been in the program long, and she wasn't sure I was ready for him, but I said, 'This dog is here for me, and I'm here for him, and I won't let you down.'"

Mugsly came in with worms, and the treatment was unpleasant, but this didn't bother Dakota:

> *The worm medicine gave him horrible poop, and I had to clean it up all the time, right away so the other dogs wouldn't get worms, too. But I didn't mind. I wanted him to get well. He was really a smart dog, and poop and all, he became the best friend I'd been wanting my whole life.*
>
> *Ms. Dalton had taken a chance on me, and that was something I'd hardly ever had in my life before. I would have done my best with Mugsly no matter what, but that someone had shown they believed in me and trusted me, which made it even more important to me to do things right by Mugsly.*

MUGSLY GETS A HOME

Dakota's efforts worked out, and within a few months, Mugsly was adopted. The boy noted,

> *It was funny how it happened. We weren't even looking for a family for him yet. A family was coming to take a look at another dog, and so all of us were out walking our dogs to meet the new family.*
>
> *Well, we got to the administration building to meet up with the family, and Mugsly saw some birds off in the distance. Don't ask me how he got off his collar, but he did, and he went tearing off after birds. The security guards were around and started yelling to get him. I called him, and he just forgot about those birds. He turned around, ran back to me, and sat down just like I taught him to do.*
>
> *The family was so impressed that they decided he was the dog for them. They wanted to take him on a home visit, so Ms. Dalton had me sit down that night and write down everything I could about him—which commands he knew, his favorite treat, how to brush him the way he liked, everything I could think of. I didn't mind doing this at all. I was like a proud parent, full of pride about how smart he was, and like a concerned parent, I wanted to make sure he was treated right and given the things he loved and deserved.*

The visit went well, and the family adopted Mugsly. Two weeks later, Dakota too, was released from MacLaren.

Sometime later, I was having brunch with a friend at a very nice hotel, and I looked up at our server, and it was Dakota. He told me, "In the eleven years I've been out, I have been clean and haven't been to jail, not even a ticket. Thanks for Project POOCH. It helped me be the man I am today and saved my life." He reminisced:

> *I will never forget Mugsly or POOCH. I have kids now, and learning about the patience and responsibility of caring for a dog has made me a patient parent. I will never be a parent like my parents were. I know love takes commitment, patience, and understanding. I give that to my kids, and I stay out of trouble because I know everything I do will affect them.*

But most of all, when I think of POOCH, I think of how I went into the program a messed-up kid full of anger and a bunch of crap, and I came out of it a man who was capable of making good decisions, caring for others, and keeping my temper in check.

12

Setting the Bar Higher

1996

Every day, I saw more learning opportunities for me and the youths. Starting each day with young people ready for any new adventure or experience was exhilarating. It was like meeting the youths with a wrapped box with a bow on top and watching their expressions, trying to guess what might be the surprise experience of the day. It was about to be another day of being happy that I had chosen teaching as a career.

I said, "Everyone, get your dogs leashed for a walk so we can come back to learn about a surprise coming your way." They scurried out of the room and were ready to do the morning walk around the large campus. Their excitement had already been transferred to their dogs, evident as they looked at their handlers and wagged their tails.

"Dogs walked, kennel runs cleaned, and dogs fed"—the dog handlers let me know they had finished the main essentials needed by their dogs. When everything was complete, I allowed them a cup of Starbucks or caffeine-free tea before I told them the good news: "Next week, a film crew from NHK in Japan will visit our program for several days." By the look on their faces, I could tell it was sinking in that they had been doing outstanding work rescuing and saving dogs.

"Really?" someone blurted out.

"Yes, really," I replied.

TD, a very tall youth, had recently joined the program, and I noticed him looking at a piece of paper one day when walking a dog. "What are you reading?" I asked. He replied, "I'm practicing Japanese to be a translator." What I had just told the group about NHK got TD's attention, so he volunteered to teach everyone a Japanese greeting to impress the visitors.

"We need to prepare before our visitors arrive," I announced. "Will someone step up to the whiteboard so we all understand what tasks we must take care of before our visitors arrive?"

PRACTICING SOCIAL MANNERS

Some protocols must be followed whenever the news media comes into the facility.

Youth must have signed releases for their likeness to be filmed, and I was responsible for meeting with the press and someone from the central office regarding what else could be filmed on campus. For example, no filming of youth elsewhere on campus.

We continued discussing and later practiced social manners and how to converse with a stranger. "What about new shirts since we will be on TV?" asked someone. That led to a discussion of what kind of shirt and color to lettering on the front.

"Bandanas for the dogs, too." I agreed to look into the request.

I brought in a world globe to show them where Japan was located. Most youth had never traveled outside Oregon except maybe across the border to Washington.

The weather forecast was to be desirable for filming outside, which meant they could set up a limited agility course to show off what the dogs could do.

"It's getting close to calling you out for a line move back to your units for lunch, but we will continue planning. Keep coming up with good ideas," I said.

After walking, training, and playing with their dogs in the afternoon, the students got busy preparing adoption flyers for their dogs.

FILM CREW FROM JAPAN ARRIVES

A week later, the film crew arrived. Everyone on campus was curious about what was going on. One of the most popular shots was coming through the sally port to get inside the fence. I found myself walking with the cameraman since I soon discovered he tried to film some of what was not allowed.

The youth were excited to move around and show off their dogs. "Hey, guys, just so you know, if you do not want to be interviewed by the film crew, you can refuse," I reminded them. There was no problem getting volunteers who wished to be interviewed.

Since the dog is tiny and the youth is tall, the youth got on his knees and was closer to the dog's eye level. (Photo from author's collection.)

I stood back as much as possible to let the youth get a chance to tell the world that regardless of why they were locked up, they were now doing something good—saving and training dogs that could have been euthanized due to behavioral issues or being overlooked at shelters.

It was remembered as one of their better days being locked up.

I soon learned that my day was not over. We usually consider a workday to be eight hours. Well, the film crew works more like twelve-hour days. After we gathered for supper, it was time to put in several more hours, giving them information for the sound bites. I went home so tired that I fell asleep in a chair. As a morning person, I returned early to MacLaren for the second day of filming. While driving, I kept thinking about how much we learn from experiencing and doing rather than just reading about things.

Sometime later, we received a copy of the finished DVD. I brought in some popcorn so the youth could have a "movie" treat while they saw themselves in action. The youth laughed when one of the dogs did great at the initial start of the agility course but veered off right before the finish. A photo of Jack, a little white dog, flashed on the screen as a youth prepared a dog flyer.

The word was out about the first on-site dog program at a juvenile correctional facility in America. NHK came back and did other films on the program. Noriko Imanishi, a popular author of middle school children's books, wrote about Project POOCH in her book, *Dog Shelter.* Her husband, a professional photographer, provided the photography. Animal Planet

The agility dog walk is placed near ground level to help the dog learn to walk confidently and then move to a higher level. Once this is mastered, the dog will learn how to maneuver other obstacles on the agility course. (Photo from author's collection.)

The youth holds a recently groomed little white dog while a flyer advertising the dog's profile is being prepared on a computer. (Photo from author's collection.)

came twice to feature the program. The youth mistakenly thought one of the producers was Jane Goodall.

JOURNALIST TEACHES WRITING

"What do you think about having me help the boys write stories for a POOCH monthly newspaper?" asked Nancy Hill, an Oregon author. The newspaper was available for free on newsstands. A few youths were on board, and she worked with them to describe interesting happenings in the program. They wrote about dog training and behavior with Nancy's guidance.

There were no boring days. The youths were anxious to practice new skills and see the results they were getting with their dogs. Adopters came to the kennel to meet the dogs and youths. The dog handlers learned how to meet a potential adopter and talk about their dog. Adopters were highly open to giving kudos to the dog handlers for how well-trained the dogs were. That was about to change for a dog named Zo.

A DOG NAMED ZO

Zo was a seventy-pound Australian shepherd/rottweiler mix. Larry, his handler, read what he had written on Zo's flyer: "I am a dog with very special needs. I do have territorial aggressive issues, and I'm currently in an intensive training program to help me with my issues. I need a home to run in, in a rural area. I need my future owner to have a significant amount of experience with dogs and be able to keep up with my training all the time, not just sometimes. All I want is someone to give me a chance in life."

I brought in a behaviorist to work with Larry and Zo. The behaviorist told Larry, "Do not let Zo sit on your foot. He warns people that you are his and they need to stay away."

A few days later, I noticed Larry was letting Zo sit on his foot. I said, "Why are you letting Zo do that? Didn't the behaviorist tell you not to?" Larry replied, "My grandmother died, and I don't have any other family. Zo is my only family." Shortly after, Zo bit a staff member. I was told Zo had to be removed from campus within twenty-four hours. I was desperate, my mind racing. What could I do to save Zo?

I tried Best Friends in Utah, but they could not take him because they had too many dogs with Zo's problems. Next, I tried a small shelter in the Portland area, Family Dogs New Life. They said they would take Zo and try to find him a home. He was in an area with other dogs for playtime during the day. I followed up several times to see how he was doing. I did site visits for confirmation. I soon got a call from the shelter, and a local farmer had come to meet Zo. The farmer was in a meet-and-greet room waiting for Zo to be brought to him. When Zo was brought into the room, Zo lunged at the farmer. The farmer said, "That's the dog for me!" As noted in a follow-up after placement, when the farmer was on his tractor in the fields, Zo trotted right alongside, which was just what the farmer had hoped would happen.

Once the dog handlers had obtained their high school diploma, they could work with the dogs for a full day. It was better for the dogs to have the same handler consistently. The dog handlers earned a small monthly

Zo bit a campus staff member and had been ordered off campus within twenty-four hours. Since the youth's grandmother had recently died, he was sad that now the dog he loved had to leave campus. (Photo from author's collection.)

wage to deposit in their trust account. To add to their monthly wage, we began boarding former POOCH dogs, which gave the youths a percentage of the proceeds. There was often a tip included. The youths had devised an idea to provide a free bath before the dog went home.

13

Dogs Bring Volunteers

The request was left in a voicemail at the kennel: "Her former owner badly abused Ginger. Please call about taking her into your program."

I arranged to go to the Willamette Humane Society and video Ginger so the youths could help decide if we could handle what Ginger might need to be adopted. Ginger's cage card listed her as a sixty-pound English pointer. I planned to return the next day to gather Ginger if the youths said yes.

The youths were seated on a donated sofa and chairs in front of the pull-down screen, ready to view the video of Ginger. After the viewing, I asked, "Do you think we can rehabilitate this dog so she will be adoptable?"

Kristofer, a POOCH youth, spoke up: "I was abused too. I want to work with Ginger and use some of the ways I am learning how to deal with my own abuse." The next day, I brought Ginger to Project POOCH. Ginger was initially terrified of Kristofer, but he just sat in a chair in the main kennel yard and let her come to him when she was ready. He didn't try to grab her.

Noriko Imanishi wrote in her book, *Dog Shelter:* "Supported by love, Ginger opened her heart to Kristofer, and as a result, the dog recovered her trust in people."

Kristofer worked on an adoption flyer featuring Ginger. I posted it in a veterinary clinic, hoping an interested adopter would call.

Karen Rake was a vet tech at the clinic where I posted the flyer. She called to say a client was interested in meeting Ginger. Karen agreed to go with Ginger and me to the home of the interested adopter. We decided that Karen would be the main spokesperson because she knew the potential adopters, Tracy Lucas and Mark Oronzo. She explained that they recently had to have their old dog euthanized at the veterinary clinic where Karen worked.

I was the adoption counselor, and all the records were in a file folder. If Tracy and Mark were interested in adopting, I would review the records with them and offer a trial overnight. Sometimes, adopters don't know until the dog spends one night if they are ready for another dog.

We left Ginger in my SUV to check out their living situation. Karen rang the doorbell as I stood nervously to the side of the door.

Tracy invited us in and offered a tour of her home and backyard. I noticed she had already set up a bowl of water in the kitchen, which was a good sign. After checking out the feasibility of the home for Ginger, Tracy asked, "Where's the dog?"

I went to get Ginger and walked her up the six steps to the front door. The look on Tracy's face was priceless. She beamed with joy and acceptance. Ginger felt it, and it was agreed that she would be fostered initially. Fostering did not last long. Mark and Tracy contacted us the next day to say they wanted to adopt Ginger.

ADOPTERS BECOME VOLUNTEERS

Soon after, Tracy and Mark visited the program and were hooked. They liked how the youths shared how good they felt saving shelter dogs. Mark and Tracy decided to take the required training to volunteer at MacLaren. Tracy often took dogs off campus to give them time out of their kennel environment, and she helped me test dogs' temperament. I showed her the Emily Weiss test when testing a dog. Mark introduced the youths to photography and showed them how to develop better adoption flyers using computer programs. Tracy and Mark did several things to help POOCH over the years, including donating to the annual fundraiser, contributing to the POOCH scholarship fund, buying the kennel's first professional bathtub, and purchasing software.

Tracy said, "We watch boys grow into men, and the transformation is deeply moving. They have all made serious mistakes, and they're paying the price, but deep down, they are good human beings."

CHURCH DEACON LISTENS TO YOUTH

People with other experiences and skill sets started volunteering to help the youths and dogs. Volunteers are priceless and are highly valued for their expertise in many areas.

When Tom Lang became a deacon in the Episcopal church, he chose incarcerated youth as his ministry. He became a Commission on Prison Ministry member, and shortly after that, the commission asked him to deliver a check to Project POOCH. Tom was often referred to as a good listener and counselor by the youths. He volunteered most Saturdays. He walked with the youths and dogs around campus. The youths liked that they could share their concerns or troubles with him, and what they said would be kept confidential. I soon learned that Tom not only liked walking with the youths, but he also liked the dogs.

While Tom and his wife had never had a dog, POOCH changed that. Tom said:

> *We had been married for thirty-seven years without a dog. Then, one day, a nine-year-old dog named Jake came along. I remember the day quite well. The youth and staff were all gathered in one room, and Jake came in and sniffed each youth for a minute or two and then went on to the next one. When he came to me, he sniffed me, then licked my nose. I was hooked. The boys trained him, and my wife and I gave him his retirement home. We had him for five years before cancer claimed him.*

I was often surprised that it wasn't always about the dog and an adopter finding each other. It can also be about people connecting.

TILLY THE DOG INTRODUCES HER HANDLER

We received an application from a couple who wanted to come to the correctional facility with their ten-year-old neurodivergent son to meet Tilly, a Labrador/shepherd mix being trained by Nathanael.

Nathanael had been in the program for eight months when Tilly arrived from a shelter. Her previous owner had given up Tilly. He said, "Tilly is a problem dog and hard to deal with, so whatever you want to do with her is fine."

A staff member at the shelter said Tilly was kept in a yard and garage because the owner was hardly ever at home. I replied, "I'll take her and find the best owner." I was already thinking that Nathanael and Tilly would be a good match. Both had high energy levels. Nathanael took to Tilly right away. When Nathanael approached her kennel run, Tilly jumped up on him as he opened the door. Without delay, Nathanael shouted sternly, "Off, Tilly!" Tilly did as she was told. Nathanael rewarded her immediately with a "good girl." It didn't take long for them to develop a strong bond with each other. Just what I had hoped for. Nathanael knew Tilly would be considered for adoption soon.

I was starting to see more than a possible dog adoption by a family when Nathanael said, "Tilly doesn't consider my past. She sees me as a man, not a robber or someone sent to reform school. I regret not only what I've done but how I used to live. I regret everything. I always blamed other people for my troubles. I always thought I was always right."

Nathanael often caused me to smile because he was good at coming up with suggestions to improve things, which was not always welcomed at a correctional facility. He had an idea to improve cleaning that we adopted. He also came up with an idea for overalls for the youths.

The day came for a new family to meet Tilly. She had been groomed and had a bandana around her neck. Along with Nathanael and Tilly, I headed to the administration building near the front of campus to meet and greet the family. The couple, Lisa, Craig, and their son, Jordan, soon arrived. Nathanael extended his hand to Lisa and Craig and encouraged Jordan to come closer and meet Tilly.

Jordan is very good at remembering numbers. He kept asking me the date of my birth. His father said, "He can remember thousands of digits, having heard them only once."

Nathanael again encouraged Jordan to come to meet Tilly. The next thing I saw was the three of them running in circles. Jordan's father said, "I have never seen Jordan be so comfortable with someone he has met for the first time. What a surprise."

Tilly found her forever home, which is why Nathanael and Jordan became pen pals. Since I had already visited Lisa and Craig's home, another home visit was unnecessary. Nathanael looked at Jordan and said, "Jordan, you can write me a letter any time you have a question about Tilly. OK?"

As Jordan and Tilly were preparing to leave, Tilly looked back at Nathanael several times as they headed out. Nathanael said, "Good luck to you," as he turned his back to Tilly, not wanting anyone to see his eyes begin to water.

Letter writing between Nathanael and Jordan was helpful to both. Nathanael was assured that Tilly was loved in her new home; Jordan, an only child, liked having Nathanael as a big brother. Jordan often asked about various commands Tilly knew but wasn't doing for him.

Jordan, an only child, saw Nathanael, the dog handler, as a big brother. They corresponded when Jordan wanted to learn how to get Tilly to follow commands. (Photo from author's collection.)

After many years, Tilly was having health problems that could not be overcome. The family decided on home euthanasia and asked me to be there at Tilly's final goodbye. It was heartbreaking to see Jordan use such beautiful words as Tilly passed. He told her, "I will always have you in my heart. I will be with you again someday." He and Tilly had developed a special bond.

14

There Was No Seat for Me at the Table

1997–1999

I was immersed in the program and added new classes for MacLaren's students. It was too late when I discovered that decisions about Project POOCH and my own future were being made behind closed doors.

I had been balancing my time with teachers and the dog program. The program was experiencing growth and seemed to be sailing smoothly in 1997. Measure 11 caused the incarcerated population to increase, and more living units were added. The administration focused on building regional facilities so youth could be closer to home. Location changes would also make it less complicated for families from the eastern part of the state. Traveling over the mountains during winter could be hazardous. Many visitors and families from a distance also had to pay for motel expenses once they got to Woodburn.

I infrequently visited correctional facilities in other states as an auditor of their education programs. The travel took me away from MacLaren for three to four days at a time.

WE ARE MOVING YOU OUT AS PRINCIPAL

Being a school administrator, I felt I was doing the work I loved and was destined to do. What a surprise when John asked to meet with me in his office for something I was unprepared to hear. "You are being moved out of the principalship to my office in Salem," he said. My world fell apart. First, I was in shock that I was receiving such an ultimatum. I tried to remain calm, but my body had tightened, and I was no longer relaxed. I felt like a caged dog being suddenly lassoed by animal control and taken to death row.

He said, "We want you to help plan the education departments in the five new regional facilities." He was silent as if waiting for me to say something. He repeated, "Your office will be in the Oregon Department of Education in Salem."

"When?" I asked. He responded, "Right away."

I felt betrayed and ostracized. I started to ask questions, but he indicated our conversation was over. I didn't want any office staff to see me in tears, so I excused myself and left campus for the day.

The layout in the Salem office was an open concept with gray portable walls to separate each worker from others. My assigned area was right outside the women's restroom. Concentrating was difficult because women would stand outside the restroom and carry on conversations.

NEW PRINCIPAL MAKES MAJOR CHANGES

After I moved to my new office in Salem, a man from Texas who had worked in a correctional facility for females took my place as principal of the high school at MacLaren. He quickly started dismantling the coffee barista training program I had started. He had moved the equipment to his previous work site. Next, he enforced a policy prohibiting dogs in the school building. He imitated kicking a dog with his foot as he laughed.

At the end of the school term, I submitted grades for the POOCH dog handlers still working on their high school credits, which he refused to accept. He wrote, "You are no longer principal and cannot submit grades." He was now the principal, and no administrator seemed interested in overriding his decision.

To say I was discouraged is an understatement—I was angry. It was not fair to take away what the boys had earned. How could I fight for the boys and their right to have their work rewarded?

I was disappointed not to be included in other major decisions. I was starting to see a pattern that concerned me. I was becoming an outsider of no importance. It was heart-wrenching to be pulled away from my role as principal. I had focused on finding positive examples of teaching as I walked into the classrooms. I would then give kudos at faculty meetings in hopes that others would desire to be singled out as doing much-needed work in sometimes difficult situations. I tried to show the teachers that I cared about them and the frustration they sometimes experienced when a fight broke out in class, or when someone said or did something inappropriate. If a teacher had enough of the student disturbance, he was sent to the office to see me. I would address the "why" and how the student could improve. After talking with the student and permitting him to return to his classroom, I would get a request: "May I have a piece of candy?" I would let him take a piece of candy from the bowl on my desk, and he happily returned to class. After a while, I learned that many students became disruptive to be sent to the office and receive candy. The candy dish disappeared. Lesson learned.

Thanksgiving was a day I wanted to show my gratitude to the teachers by having a catered lunch in the library. A nearby restaurant agreed to prepare box lunches along with a dessert. I had asked for an RSVP since I paid for the lunches. Luckily, I remembered running short of cookies at the grand opening of the POOCH program. I added additional lunches in case a teacher showed up without an RSVP. Sure enough, two teachers came from the compound area separate from the main high school, saying they heard a free lunch was available.

Giving teachers opportunities to attend conferences and workshops to show my support for their learning from other educators was something I valued as a teacher. The conferences also allowed the teachers to talk with other professionals from alternative and public schools. Additionally, I was adamant about teachers following the agreed-upon union contract; however, there were times when I needed to advise them of situations of inappropriateness with students. The union representative would then develop a defense in favor of the teacher. I wondered if this was why I was removed as principal.

Of course, not being on-site to experience outcomes from the youths working with dogs brought me to tears when I drove home at the end of the day.

INFORMING YOUTHS

I didn't want to leave the dog handlers wondering why I wasn't showing up at the kennel, so I squeezed time in on the weekends to let them know what was happening. Too many people in their lives had let them down, and I wasn't going to be one of them. I showed up on the weekends since the education budget covered Monday through Friday only. After lunch on Saturday, we sat in the education center to discuss the changes being made. I told them we would focus on getting homes for the few dogs waiting to be adopted. The program's teaching assistant quit when he learned he would not receive any benefits. The youths were stunned that what they had heard on campus was true. I kept telling myself I needed to be strong. "I am here to answer any of your questions or concerns," I said. I let them know I would continue to advocate for them and their dogs. I encouraged them to think about questions or concerns I could address when I returned on Sunday. "If you have a family visit on Sunday, send your questions and concerns with another dog handler," I told them. Someone mentioned that my leaving was like being told suddenly by a foster parent that they were being sent to a new foster home. As I walked them back to their living units, I let them know I would work on how to get through the disappointment all of us were experiencing. When I arrived to take them to the kennel on Sunday, a youth handed me a card that read, "Thank you, Ms. D, for all you have done for us!! We all appreciate everything you do!! We've never known a more giving person or someone who cares about others more than you. Let us know how we can help."

After reading the note, I knew getting the program back was my highest priority. My world had crumbled, but now I needed a plan. I would strategically consider how to continue making a big difference in the lives of the youths and dogs.

PROGRAM SHUTS DOWN

At the most inopportune time the next week, I received a notification from human resources in the Oregon Department of Education. It was a layoff notice a year after the regional education programs were ready for students. The human resources at the Department of Education knew I had been a Title IX coordinator; I believe they thought it best to, at the same time, lay off a white male and a Black male. The two males had been blindsided, too.

It was July, and families often wanted to adopt a dog because their children were out of school for the summer. A dog could keep children busy and help them learn to be responsible. Dog adoptions were completed, and no new dogs came in. I tried not to display my sadness. The door had closed.

There was now a new principal, and I had received a layoff notice, but I continued to talk with the new superintendent, Gary Lawhead, about staffing for Project POOCH. The new principal had already indicated that he was not interested in continuing the program.

NEVER GIVE UP HOPE

I no longer had a job but continued volunteering at POOCH by conducting administrative paperwork, making presentations in Europe and Asia, fundraising, and never giving up hope.

In October 1999, the principal agreed to provide a full-time teaching assistant out of his budget for Project POOCH. The future looked bright again, and the POOCH youths would have dogs.

I added transportation of out-of-state visitors to the kennel as an additional responsibility. I also met with the youths once a week to include them in the next steps and how they could be involved. I was so proud of them. They were sometimes a little down, not knowing what would happen to the program, but they kept busy fulfilling their responsibilities and learning about dogs through videos and speakers. I often told them that life involves solving problems and hoping for positive outcomes. I continued strategizing to get the program back since John would pay for a person to supervise at the kennel five days a week. Weekends were still a question.

I was in a bit of a predicament without a job. One of my mentors encouraged me to apply for school administrator positions. I got right to the task and soon had an interview in which I was offered the position of school principal in a public school. I needed to do my homework before I accepted. I called the current principal the next day and asked, "What has been your experience working in this school?"

Without hesitation, he said, "You don't want the position; the parents are always trying to run the school." He gave examples in which it appeared that there were often no boundaries between parents and the school.

A few days later, I had given the principalship much thought and decided I had found my passion in working with troubled youth in the criminal justice system. I declined the offer.

I did consulting work for local businesses and workshops for administrative support personnel; however, it was not enough income to keep me afloat. It was time to be bold and take a risk, so I put my house on the market. My POOCH dog, Sasha, sat on the front porch and enjoyed watching library patrons across the street. I was anxious and sad that I had no other option but to sell the first house I had purchased on my own if I wanted to keep Project POOCH alive.

A real estate agent I had worked with when I purchased the house came forward to help me sell it. My business professor mentor offered to pay my mortgage until the house sold. I was ecstatic that someone believed in me enough to make such an offer, and of course, I accepted. The agent had assured me the house was in an excellent location and would sell even though the market had slowed down. She held an open house that other real estate agents attended. A few potential buyers from California visited. One was a young woman who made it known how much she loved the place. "It's just what I am looking for," she said.

I was elated that it looked like I would sell the house soon. The agent was also happy about what looked to be a sale.

Everything changed the next day when the potential buyer contacted the agent and said, "I have some extensive dental work to be done, so I will not be making an offer."

My real estate agent tried to encourage me not to get discouraged. "The right family will come along," she said. She was right. A local couple with two children liked the location of my house and bought it. Things were beginning to turn around. I had an idea of the best way to keep moving forward.

15

New Experiences

1999–Forward

LEARNING HOW TO LEAD A NONPROFIT

Since I incorporated Project POOCH as a nonprofit in late 1998, I needed to learn how to run a successful nonprofit. I started taking classes at Portland State University on managing a nonprofit organization. I began assembling a stellar board of directors with experienced businesspeople who believed in second chances for young men and dogs.

In 1999, it was time to reopen Project POOCH. I had come this far and had documented evidence that the program worked. I was determined to move forward and stabilize the program with a new model for continued success. Donors were willing to make large donations because they could now get a tax write-off. We also had enough money to rent an off-site administrative office. MacLaren's administration did not want donations coming to the correctional facility. There needed to be a separation. They would partner with us but keep the financial part of the nonprofit located off-site for precautionary reasons.

There was also a new superintendent at MacLaren. Superintendent Jester had retired, and Gary Lawhead had taken over. He continued supporting Project POOCH and agreed to fund a staff member five days a week. The board of directors had allowed POOCH to fund an approved corrections staff member for weekends.

BOARD MEMBERS VISIT THE KENNEL AND PROVIDE SUPPORT

A board member, Stan Bland, stepped up to fund a part-time office assistant at an off-campus site. Other board members donated and got their friends to donate. "What can be better than donors saving boys and dogs?" they asked when requesting others give.

Several board members were fathers with grown sons and had experience dealing with young males. The same was true of some consistent donors. I was beyond excited to start the program again, and people stepped forward to support the cause financially and as volunteers. I invited board members to the kennel to learn more about the kind of dogs we were bringing in from shelters so they could meet the young men in the program. The young men practiced their social skills by offering the board members coffee, tea, or water. They passed around a tin of cookies and napkins.

CARLOS SHARES HIS STORY

Several days before the event, Carlos had volunteered to tell his story . He had written out his speech, and I had found a lectern for him to speak from. He said:

> *Good morning. My name is Carlos, and I want to share my story with you. I was born in Mexico and came to the United States with my parents, brother, and sister. My father and mother were hard workers. They were proud of the grades I got in school. I helped my family in the fields and was liked by others.*
>
> *My family moved to another town when I was younger, and I joined a gang. I began stealing, fighting, drinking, smoking pot, and selling drugs. The police knew who I was. I was bad and shot another gang member trying to defend my brother.*

I could sense some uneasiness from Carlos when he told the board what he had done to end up at MacLaren, so I smiled and thanked him for being willing to share his story. "Now, Carlos is going to get his dog and show you how he is doing some good work to help his dog get adopted," I said.

He brought in his dog, Chico, and gave commands in Spanish. That amazed everyone. "I wanted my dog to be bilingual, like me," said Carlos. Everyone laughed.

"It's about time for the dog handlers to feed their dogs and then return to their living units for lunch," I explained.

The dog handlers shook hands with the board members and thanked them for coming. I could tell the experience had opened the board members' eyes. They were impressed with the behavior of the dog handlers and their dogs. We learned many worthwhile ways of enriching and improving the program because people came forward to provide input and much-needed skills. Pet supply stores offered fundraisers, donated quality dog food, and kept donation boxes on their counters.

I believe the program worked because the young men made it work. We would not have a successful program if they did not maintain high standards for themselves and the dogs. They loved working with dogs and wanted to be responsible. They kept a chart on every dog to indicate when medications were given and food dispersed. Any unusual dog behaviors were reported to a kennel supervisor.

In 2000, Oregon's Governor John Kitzhaber awarded one of the boys who worked for POOCH a Youth Making a Difference Award. The youth had graduated from Western Oregon University with a degree in criminal justice.

Once a youth had completed his time and was released from corrections, I often gave him some pocket money to help tell the POOCH story at fundraisers. The adult volunteers at the same events learned how to answer

The youth has just been assigned a boxer dog, who will sit next to him as he reads the dog's records (vaccinations and behaviors) from the animal shelter. (Photo from author's collection.)

questions by listening to the youth describe how the program worked and how to adopt a program dog.

Later in the program, we were invited to show visuals of Project POOCH at an annual purebred dog show. We always had at least two volunteers at the table so one person could walk around and see dogs in judging rings and being groomed.

One weekend, while at the POOCH table, I returned to see a visitor haranguing our youth volunteer by repeatedly asking what he did to get locked up. I was proud of the youth for keeping his cool. I stepped in, introduced myself, and explained that the youth had done his time and was at the event to talk about the program, not what he did to get locked up. She listened and quietly walked away.

Through newsletters, events, and media attention, the program became well-known. Other rescuers sought our help taking dogs they had recently brought in from other states but needed help housing. We were getting some dogs from the state of Washington and rescues from the south due to severe flooding. Since we could not temperament test dogs arriving from other states, we had to trust that we were getting accurate information about dogs seeking placement with POOCH.

Shortly before Hurricane Katrina hit Louisiana in 2005, I sent our administrative assistant, Brie Caffey, to volunteer rescue training at a dog shelter in Oregon. She was happy to go to the two-day training. Before she was to return to our community outreach office, she called to say there was a Labrador at the dog shelter where she was getting training. "Do I have permission to bring him to Project POOCH?" she asked.

"Bring him in," I replied.

SAVING HURRICANE KATRINA DOGS

Although Brie did not go to help the animals after Hurricane Katrina, she did help bring two Katrina dogs from another rescue to us. She had received a call at our outreach office about two forty-pound dogs that needed help. "The dogs appeared to be siblings. They were all black and looked like a mixed breed," she said.

"Can you get a photo?" I asked. "I want to get input from the youth in POOCH."

When we got the photo, I went to the kennel to see what the youth thought about bringing in the dogs. Kyle spoke up about being separated from his sister in foster care: "My mother could not care for us, so my grandmother did the best she could, but she died. I began getting in trouble with the law. Let's take both dogs and find them a home together. I know they will be happier together than separated."

The youth named the dogs Bert and Ernie.

A young couple came to meet Bert and Ernie. After hearing the backstory, the couple agreed that the dogs should be adopted together. Everyone was happy.

Unfortunately, the kennel received a call from the adopters the next day: "We just can't handle both dogs." They kept Ernie and brought back Bert.

We were disappointed about the failed adoption until we got another call from relatives of the young couple. "We want to adopt Bert. The dogs will live in different homes but can have frequent playdates," they said. Now, we were all happy for the dogs again.

Although I was now taking nonprofit classes in the evenings and attending breakfast meetings to network with others working in nonprofits, I realized we needed revenue we could count on. I learned that big donors like to see the financials of nonprofits to understand how much is spent on overhead and the top administrator's salary. Donors like to see the most significant percentage of income going to the program, not wages.

Since the superintendent had agreed to pay for staffing five days a week, I set up an interview committee. This time, I was seated at the table and helped interview interested applicants. Some staff thought walking around campus with well-vetted youth and their dogs would be easy. It was ideal to hire someone with experience at MacLaren and a solid understanding of corrections rules to supervise the youths and dogs in the program.

Sometimes, visitors pass contraband to the incarcerated. The most frequent item we had to watch out for at the kennel was pornography on DVDs. Searches were done regularly at the living units of the incarcerated and at work sites. Sometimes, security would get information that a student was viewing something inappropriate online; they would come to the kennel after hours and go through everything, including the computers. They didn't realize that our computers at the kennel were not connected

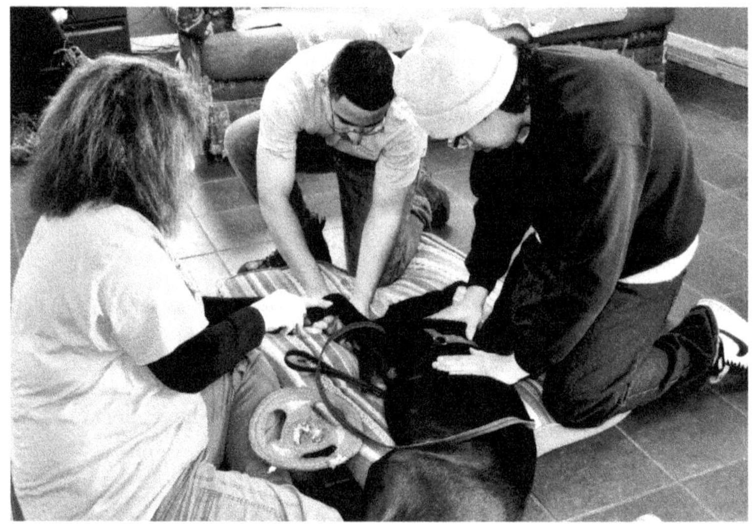

The dog massage therapist placed the dog on a heavy blanket on the tile floor in the kennel education room. She first demonstrated key areas of the dog's body that need attention. The youths practiced dog massage. (Photo from author's collection.)

Roxanne, the yoga teacher, came once a week to teach the youth yoga poses and breathing techniques, showing them that they were in control of their bodies and breath and had self-calming tools. (Photo from author's collection.)

to the Internet. Of course, such searches after hours set the dogs off in a barking frenzy.

We became a cohesive family as everyone became more knowledgeable about dogs and their care. The young men in the program were intense and followed directions when the veterinarian asked for assistance holding a dog for microchipping, vaccinations, and checking for lameness. They loved using the stethoscope to check their heart and their dog's heart. Dog massage was very new to the program participants. They weren't allowed to give massages to each other, so yoga became a way for them to relax and be calm. Roxanne came weekly to work with the young men as they learned from a certified yoga instructor. She always brought her canine companion for independence, Monarch, to hang out during class. Monarch seemed to know when a youth was not in the right space and would lie next to him during class.

An attorney brought a video and talked to the dog handlers about animal abuse and Oregon's law enforcement. It was an intense discussion, and a lot of questions were asked. Understanding the difference between neglect and abuse with examples was useful.

Pet first aid was a half-day class so that everyone could earn certification. I would meet the trainer at the campus entrance and transport stuffed dogs to the kennel for the training.

A young man came to me one morning and wanted me to know his birthday was coming up on Saturday. Since my mother always made our birthdays important by letting my siblings and me choose what flavor cake and frosting we wanted on our big day, I decided to start bringing a cake on birthdays. They and their dogs would wear dollar store hats while we sang "Happy Birthday." Seeing how much everyone liked being remembered on their birthday brought me much joy.

One day, when I asked a young man what kind of cake he wanted for his birthday, he answered, tres leche. On my way home, I stopped at Senor Lopez's restaurant and asked if he could provide the requested cake. When I picked up the cake a few days later, I was surprised at the price. I had to watch our social budget because now we had started getting the exact same request from others. I also added goodbye cakes when boys were being released from corrections.

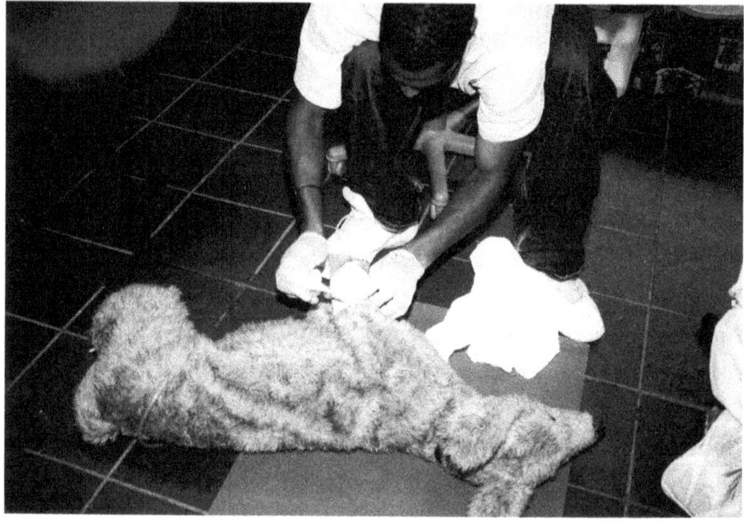

A certified pet first aid instructor brought stuffed dogs, bandages, and a booklet for each student to learn how to care for an injured dog. A youth is practicing bandaging a dog's leg. The instructor checks to make sure the bandages aren't too tight. The student is wearing latex gloves to keep his hands clean. (Photo from author's collection.)

The board of directors often asked me questions about the program participants, so I initiated an annual holiday party in the canteen located in the administration building. I told the young men that each boy would be paired with a board member. Before the meal, they would introduce their assigned board member to the group. They would need to have a conversation with their assignee and ask questions so they would have something to say about someone other than their name. "Like, what questions should we ask about them?" someone asked. I replied, "Don't ask anything personal. Ask if they have pets and then ask what they like about them. If they don't have pets, find out if they have ever had one and what their experience was like." I cautioned them to be prepared if their assigned guest asked about the dog they were training for adoption. At the end of the holiday meal, the young men thanked the board members for spending time with them and learning more about the program. Each board member received a Project POOCH sweatshirt. After the young men were escorted back to the kennel to care for their dogs, I chatted with board members.

They were impressed that the young men were learning social skills and training shelter dogs for their forever home.

Given the chance, the incarcerated in the program want to be better people and be able to visualize a future with a job as a good neighbor in their community. They need guidance on how to make that happen.

16

Don't Shoot the Dog

My social life became extremely limited while taking nonprofit classes, developing a program vision and goals, and helping select dogs and young men for the program. It was not a nine-to-five job with weekends off, but I was driven to lead the program with the help of others.

Seldom could I predict what problem might surface that needed to be addressed. For example, I was in the exam room at my doctor's office when I received a call from an adopter. He bellowed, "Come and get this dog, or I am going to shoot it! The dog bit me when I hugged a lady from the church."

I urgently said, "Open your door from the kitchen to the garage and encourage the dog to go there. I'm on my way." I hurriedly told the doctor I had an emergency and left.

About a month before, this adopter, who had recently lost his wife, had come to POOCH looking for a dog. He liked Lilly, a yellow Labrador retriever, but we did not think it was the right fit. The man said, "That dog just looks into my eyes, and we have made a connection."

With some hesitation, I volunteered to do the home visit to see if the adopter and Lilly would work out. The home had a fully fenced backyard and plenty of room for a sixty-pound dog. I spent forty-five minutes with the man, reviewing all the commands and precautions when adding a dog to the household. I then left after he had signed the adoption contract.

Several weeks later, a woman from the church went to visit him and help with his grief over losing his wife. When she went to leave the home and hugged the man, Lilly bit the man's hand.

I rushed to help. The man's hand was bleeding when I got there, so I offered to take him to the hospital, but he would have none of it. "My son is on his way over," he said.

I headed to the garage to retrieve the dog and noticed a rifle nearby. Yep, he was serious when he said he would shoot the dog.

IS LILLY DANGEROUS?

On the way back to the kennel with Lilly, I stopped at an animal emergency clinic I'd been to. They weren't busy, so I asked if a veterinarian could come out and give me Lilly's temperament assessment. Although all dogs were given a temperament test when we got them from the shelter, sometimes issues arose once they settled in the new environment. The veterinarian gave a good report and did not consider Lilly dangerous.

Not long after returning to the kennel, a family came to meet Lilly. The youth handler followed all the commands so the family could continue Lilly's training. Lilly went right to the children in the family, which sealed the deal. A weekend visit followed, and the adoptive parents signed the final adoption papers. It is good social training for the youth when they can meet an adoptive family and show what their dog has learned.

MICROCHIPPING PROTOCOLS

Months had passed since Lilly's adoption. The man with the rifle left a message on the answering machine at the kennel. "I thought I told you to get rid of that damn dog," he yelled.

Lilly had escaped from the new family, and animal control had picked her up. I had failed to change ownership of Lilly on the microchip when I took her from the man with the rifle. It was a tough lesson for me that I shared with the dog handlers.

We always hoped each dog would find the perfect home after the youths had focused on getting every dog well trained, but sometimes our hopes were dashed, and we were disappointed. We discovered that owners relinquishing a dog to a shelter did not always tell the truth about why their dog was being surrendered. We then found out the hard way, which could be stressful for everyone. If a dog did not work out, we wanted to know why so we could correct any undesirable behavior before attempting another adoption. However, we don't always get the call to bring the dog back to Project POOCH. Such was the case when, months later, I sent out a customer survey to adopters. One question was, "If applicable, please tell us in a few sentences where the dog is now and if you adopted it out to another family." One adopter answered, "Ernie is an AWESOME pet! I have never been a 'dog person,' but the husband and children really, really wanted a dog. Ernie's first adopted parents must have been [expletive] because they left this amazing animal at a shelter and never even bothered to let Project POOCH know! He obviously was not fed enough by them or cared for properly. I love this dog in a way I never thought I could ever love a dog."

We thought Ernie was still with the original family who had adopted him. I was seething about this dog being dumped in a shelter rather than contacting Project POOCH to take him back. Although Project POOCH is the secondary contact on all microchips, the shelter did not try our organization's name and number to let us know he had been given up.

Volunteer Denise Mason oversaw microchip records, and she started adding my phone number so I could be notified if someone called when the office was closed. She had been a special education teacher in public schools and always kept incredibly detailed records of all the dogs she selected from the shelters and their microchip information.

It disappoints everyone in the program when adoptions don't work out. I was looking for ways to help the boys feel less stressed when things don't go as hoped.

DEVELOPING CALM WITH YOGA

I called Roxanne and asked if she could come more often to help the youth work on their minds through their bodies with yoga guidance. She had taught street yoga (people unhoused on Portland streets can practice yoga at a local church). She always brought her CCI (Canine Companions for Independence) dog, Monarch. The CCI organization is based in California and sends its dogs to puppy raisers, who return the puppies at an agreed-upon time to learn more about working with someone experiencing a disability. I wondered what else might help the boys.

We had unused space next to our education building. I thought it looked like a good place for a meditation garden. A youth feeling a need for some time alone could bring his dog to the area and get away from the busyness of the kennel. I am not a gardener, but Denise saw the area and volunteered her skills. A couple of the young men liked the idea of helping to add to the shade tree planted when we moved the kennel from the area near the high school to the present location.

Before long, Susie Waki, my administrative assistant, her husband, and her son visited the kennel and handed me a check for the program. I

The meditation garden was just outside a window of the education building. It was a place where the youth and his dog could find some quiet time away from the busyness of kennel activity. Engraved stones with messages and heartfelt thoughts from donors filled the walkway. (Photo from author's collection.)

decided to purchase a permanent bench with the names of her husband's deceased parents on it for placement in the garden. It became a place of calm for the young men and their dogs. We added pavers that people could purchase and decide what words they wanted to put on them. The youth decided that we needed to add bird feeders so they could listen and watch the birds as they worked on their computers. The meditation garden also became a place to spread ashes when a dog died of natural causes.

WHAT ABOUT PIT BULLS?

In the beginning years of Project POOCH, we excluded pit bulls due to undercover dogfighting in Portland. Many gang members were also attracted to the breed. When I saw so many pit bulls in the shelters, I asked the MacLaren administration their thoughts. They agreed it would be okay to thoroughly test the dogs before bringing them into the program.

A large pit bull, Rocky, passed the test and became a favorite because of his sweet temperament. One day, he fainted in the meditation garden. The youths helped me load him in our donated POOCH van to get him to the

Woodburn Veterinary Clinic. He was diagnosed with cancer throughout his body. "Do I have enough time to return him to the kennel so the youth can say goodbye?" I asked Dr. Debbie Unrau. I took Rocky back to get hugs and last farewells before I returned him to the veterinary clinic. It was difficult for the youth to hold back tears. One said, "You always tell us never to give up hope. We all thought he would be okay."

We held a memorial service for Rocky in the meditation garden. Prayer flags flew on the fence, and board member Tom Lang said a prayer. We listened to the "In the Arms of the Angels" song and then spread Rocky's ashes. There was a somber feeling in the air, so we went inside and sat in the Education Center while looking at photos of Rocky on the computer and talking about how he was a good dog. I brought dog and human ice cream, a nice treat on a warm but sad day.

17

Learning New Skills and Facing New Challenges

On more than one occasion, I told the young men, "Your dog loves you no matter what you have done, what you look like, or what you smell like. Notice how your dog jumps joyfully when they see you first thing in the morning and know you are getting them out of their kennels for a walk around campus." I knew they got it when they smiled. I realized that Project POOCH youths were often experiencing unconditional love for the first time in their lives. The young men gradually developed a calmness that took the place of anxiety, hopelessness, and depression from being locked away in a correctional facility.

I immediately addressed any concerns they expressed, sometimes whether I had heard anything about how their dog was doing in their new home. "I'll contact the adopter and let you know," I would respond. I knew the emptiness one can feel when a beloved pet is gone.

CURLY IS LOST

One weekend, the Avid microchip company called about a dog named Curly, who was registered with Project POOCH.

I realized Denise had placed Curly for adoption, so I called her for more information. She remembered Curly; however, the adopter, an elderly woman, had changed his name to Juicy. The woman had moved to another town where she had been placed in assisted living.

The person from Avid said Curly was in the Jackson County Animal Shelter in Phoenix, Oregon, which is close to the Oregon/California border. I called the shelter to find out how Curly ended up so far from his original owner. The assisted living personnel had put the dog in a shelter, where a boy's mom adopted Curly for her son, who was on the autism spectrum. When the mother drove to the school with Curly to pick up her son, the dog got out and could not be found. A search was launched in the pouring rain for the little poodle mix with no luck. Someone else found the little dog and took him to the animal shelter, where his photo and information were posted on their website. The shelter said he had been examined by a veterinarian and had little sight. "If he is not reunited with his adopters, I will arrange to pick up Curly when the hold period is up," I said.

Because of my dogs, I could not go down and back in one day to get Curly, so I arranged for a retired teacher friend, Bill Caffey, to drive down on a Friday and stay all night. He said he would be at the shelter when they opened on Saturday to get Curly. Bill picked up Curly as promised and let me know when he would arrive at our meet up point to hand over Curly. When we met, my first look at Curly was not pretty. Curly was in a dog crate, and he was a mess. The shelter had bathed him, but it looked like he might have cataracts. Complete grooming was in order, too.

I called Denise again and told her I was going to her house since we agreed to have her foster him rather than take him to the kennel. When I arrived, she came out to look at Curly. "Do you think he has a chance?" she asked.

"Can you keep him overnight and take him to the vet tomorrow for an assessment?" I asked. She agreed it was a promising idea to get a professional opinion.

The next day, Denise called to say, "Curly is about 90 percent blind." We figured he was thirteen years old. Denise planned to call her groomer, Karen Rake, to get Curly cleaned up and groomed as soon as possible. Once Karen had groomed Curly, he looked ready to be shown at a dog show.

Denise's idea to foster turned into, "I'm keeping him." Her six-year-old granddaughter loved Curly and walked him on Denise's property. Since Denise has had a career as a special education teacher, she began teaching her granddaughter about people and dogs with special needs. I informed the young men in the program about Curly's situation and that the microchip was traced to Project POOCH. Curly found a new home with Denise.

TRADESPEOPLE INVOLVE YOUTH IN BUILDING NEW KENNEL RUNS

Since the young men had voiced a desire to help more dogs, I announced that Frank and Julie Jungers had donated money for us to build four new kennels with heated floors for the winter season. It would be another

Donors Frank and Julie Jungers came forward to pay for an additional four dog spaces. The youth learned how to lay bricks, and the facility electrician did the work for the heated floors in the kennel. Each kennel had a back gate facing the meditation garden. (Photo from author's collection.)

project in which the young men would learn new skills, like laying bricks for the outer part of the new kennel runs. "We want windows on the doors so the dogs can see out," said one young man.

"Will someone go to the whiteboard and write suggestions so we can talk to the tradespeople leading the project?" I asked. "We aim to finish the project before the rains come in November."

It was interesting to observe the young men who preferred working outside and those who preferred working inside. This was one way for them to learn what kind of work they might like to do in the future.

Jane Turville, an architect, had helped us with the Education Center and would help again. She had the contacts to find tradespeople willing to work on a project in corrections. Some work had to be coordinated with the Youth Authority and its electricians, plumbers, and grounds employees. Everyone enjoyed learning by doing.

I felt elated when the tradespeople told me how great it was to work with the young people in the program. The young men were learning how to work as a team and follow directions from the experts. We met our goal and had another celebration with lots of cake and accolades. They were always up for a party as a reward for doing good work and completing a project; however, I wanted them to participate in the festivities—especially presenting to strangers.

"You guys are going to be speaking at this party," I said. A few had that "not me" look on their faces. At the celebration, they were to speak first to relax and enjoy showing the visitors their completed work. They were relieved but smiled when their speaking part was done. Then came the unanticipated surprise. Anthony, the first POOCH youth, came forward and gave me an award with the following imprinted on it: *Joan Dalton, in appreciation and recognition for your outstanding support and encouragement. Anthony Washington, September 27, 2003.* I sure never saw that one coming.

STRAY CATS APPEAR

The program ran smoothly with administration, corrections staff, and maintenance support. The maintenance staff often helped us out. One day, as I was approaching the kennel, one of the maintenance crew motioned for me to come to talk with him. "Do you know we are finding stray cats down here?" he asked. I didn't. I knew where to get a couple of traps and let him know we would work on the situation. I had experience trapping feral cats and taking them to the Feral Cat Coalition of Oregon to be neutered and spayed before being returned to where they had been found. I gathered the young men together for a meeting on how to manage another kennel situation—trapping and saving feral cats. The young men would need to find out where the cats hung out and get traps correctly set and covered so they could catch them. It was good to see maintenance staff and the kennel supervisors lending their help to the unfortunate situation we now had to contend with daily.

My job was to contact people in my network who could help place any cats showing a liking to and socialization with humans. I contacted friends and acquaintances in veterinary clinics and cat rescues, as well as Karen Rake, a dog and cat groomer who had also worked as a veterinary technician. She got on with the task right away.

I took photos of the young men holding and cuddling the kittens. Karen showed her clients. She was successful and even placed one with her adult brother.

When Jay, one of the dog handlers, was not caring for dogs, he took on the task of keeping count of how many cats and kittens he had helped

The youth saved the kittens and mother cat using a humane trap with a spring-like door to catch them. The trap was metal with a handle on the top. Tuna was put in the trap to catch the kittens. They were then rehomed. The youth loved holding the kittens and handled them with compassion. (Photo from author's collection.)

save. Others joined in, and the competition was on. To see the young men smile when a kitten they placed on their heart started purring was a bonus reaction. It was pure, unconditional love, and they felt it.

Sometimes, the young men were slightly discouraged when they showed up at the kennel, and no cat was in the trap. "Well, let's keep trying. Sometimes cats shy away from the trap and aren't willing to go in," I said.

We were finally making progress finding homes for almost every trapped cat; however, the few not finding placement were now neutered or spayed and could hang out where they were found without adding to the cat population. Word somehow got out that cats were being saved at Project POOCH. Calls started coming in from people wanting us to find homes for their cats and kittens. We had to direct them to cat rescues and the few shelters taking in cats.

I wanted to find a way to recognize Jay for his leadership and tenacity in helping with the cat situation. I arranged for the superintendent to stop his weekly meeting with his staff to give an award to Jay for his successful record of trapping, caring for, and helping save cats and kittens. The award was to be a surprise, so I put on my serious face and said to Jay, "The superintendent wants to see you. I don't know what it's about, but I am escorting you to the administration building to find out."

I could tell Jay was nervous being escorted to the second floor of the administration building to meet with the superintendent. When we arrived, twelve people sat around a long table. Superintendent Dan Berger got up, approached Jay, and shook his hand. He put the award around Jay's neck like a winner at the Olympics. He then spoke about how impressed he was with Jay's compassion in saving the stray cats. Everyone clapped, and Jay was happy over the surprise visit. Jay had safely caught twenty cats and kittens. He told the group, "The cats were taken to the vet to be spayed and neutered before going to good homes."

Getting the full support of superintendents Robert Jester, Gary Lawhead, and Dan Berger was extremely important in the program's success.

18

More Incredible People Elevate POOCH

BOARD MEMBER STAN BLAND VISITS

New projects and fresh, supportive volunteers brought skills, such as Photoshop for developing dog flyers, how to present their dogs to adopters, development of social skills, and how to answer questions from potential adopters, to incarcerated young men and their dogs. Exciting times were around the corner, and I was elated beyond words.

One such person was Stan Bland. Stan and his wife, Dixie, had raised three sons. He also had a history of volunteering and serving on the boards of nonprofits with missions that involved improving the lives of children. Stan said, "When I saw POOCH, I was overwhelmed. Joan had assigned a boy about eighteen years old as my contact. He introduced himself and his dog to me. He treated his dog like a friend, telling me the dog's name, age, and breed. He was well-mannered. I was amazed by how polite this young man was, how well-spoken."

Stan left the correctional facility in disbelief about what he'd seen and heard during his visit. As we walked to the parking lot, Stan said, "The program consists of teaching kids far more than how to train and treat a dog, although that alone is enormous. They learn interpersonal skills like conducting themselves, greeting the public, and talking to people they might not normally encounter. There are projects underway where they learn new skills. They'll leave with skills they can walk away with, things they can use in their jobs when they leave."

Not long after the visit, I asked Stan if he'd like to join the board. He readily agreed and became a very active board member. He said, "Being with dogs and turning youth around is exciting." I liked it when he said, "I understand mistakes and bad timing. I didn't know what the young men had done to get in trouble, but making mistakes wouldn't be hard. These aren't bad kids. They were kids caught doing something bad, whether by choice or association."

Stan has seen nothing but positive interaction between the young men and their dogs, as well as each other. He noted, "The kids have a lot of pride, and that comes from the fact that they give things to their dogs that the dogs haven't had before, and at the same time, they're getting things from the dogs they haven't had—things like love, trust, accountability, and responsibility." Another thing Stan mentioned as valuable was learning patience and consistency. He said, "Some of these kids already have kids of their own, and patience and consistency are very important in their roles as parents."

One of the memorable events involving Stan was "Christmas in the Canteen." I had arranged a catered lunch with all the youths and board members seated at long tables that joined facing others in the room. Each young man was assigned a board member and, in some cases, the board member's spouse to learn about and then stand up and introduce the person to the entire group. I wanted to complete the introductions before the meal because I didn't want the young men to be stressed while eating. After our luncheon, each board member was given a POOCH sweatshirt.

Stan announced, "Santa brought something for the dogs." The young men didn't see anything for the dogs until Stan motioned for everyone to follow him outside. He had placed a huge box of dog toys in front of the administration building. The young men immediately started going through the box, having fun with squeaky toys and determining which dogs would get certain toys.

As a long-standing board member, Stan had seen many graduates from the program. He shared some of his thoughts: "One of the most important things the kids learn is communication skills. They are living among peers and learning interpersonal skills that help them build positive relationships. Many come from unfortunate backgrounds, but the POOCH kids leave with the understanding that they're important. Many haven't experienced love, warmth, or the care of a real friendship, but they find that at POOCH."

Although women have played major volunteer roles for the young men in the program, the male volunteers were often the only positive male role models for them.

NETWORKING

Board member Suzanne McKim introduced me to Charlie Allis. I discovered that current board members were best at knowing others for whom Project POOCH would continue to expand and progress. Charlie would stop by the kennel while he was out for a bicycle ride. He always showed interest in what the young men were doing. Charlie had talked to a friend of his, Frank Jungers, about donating money to build some additional dog runs. Charlie liked to see the progress made on the dog runs and let Frank know how his donation was being spent. Since Charlie was skilled at teaching the young men basic money-handling skills, such as learning the difference between needs and wants, and he was delighted to help them develop financial literacy.

JALEN'S STORY

As Jalen listened to Charlie, he realized he could learn something about his area of interest—finance. Jalen's homelife left a great deal to be desired. His parents divorced when he was in elementary school. His mother made no effort to conceal her preference for her older son, and Jalen was shuffled between his mother's home in Oregon and his grandparents' home in the Midwest. His father had little to do with him. Jalen coped by being the class clown and seeking approval and attention for negative behavior. He was arrested when he was fifteen for shooting a gun out of a car window. Since Jalen had joined the dog program, he had started thriving with Charlie's help.

Charlie had three grown sons and began helping with job interviews, handling money, and being a good listener. He always praised Jalen and the other students in the program when he saw them training their dogs. Charlie became the closest person to a dad that Jalen had ever had. He would arrive on Saturdays and tell Jalen, "Show me what you have taught your dog."

Additionally, Jalen looked forward to Charlie's lessons in finance. "I wanted to learn, and Charlie was willing to help me. He would teach me things I didn't know—he gave me hope," said Jalen. Charlie took the time with Jalen, and having an adult pay attention to him was something he had never experienced.

Jalen had developed a connection with Jazzy, a German shepherd mix. Jazzy was a lot like my program dog, Sasha—she had a high prey drive and was prone to escape, which is why her first adoption failed. Jalen was not discouraged. He was happy she had come back. And she was happy to be back with Jalen. The second adoption worked, and Jazzy became the symbol of the signage on our agility center named after Charlie. The logo is Jazzy jumping through a hoop titled Champs Agility Center. Charlie was a grandpa to many young men, so they combined that word with his name to devise *Champs*.

Sadly, Charlie developed a brain tumor. Every Saturday, I would take a voice recording from the young men and play it for him when he was in hospice. He, in turn, would send back a recorded message. On one such Saturday, I walked into the lobby of the hospice center to see one of Charlie's sons reading a book. He looked up when I greeted him. He said, "Dad is almost gone, but go in and see him." I headed to Charlie's room and saw he was about to leave this world. His eyes were open, but he was not aware of my presence. I whispered in his ear, "We love you." I then left and told the young men the next day that Charlie had died. They were devastated.

19

Compassion and the Incarcerated

Through their journey in Project POOCH, the young men experienced support from their peers and others when a rooster, dog, or person died. However, we experienced many heartwarming events as well.

A LOST BABY BIRD

It was the start of a spring day as I walked to the kennel. Upon arrival, the kennel supervisor, Elray Sampson, motioned me to follow him to the meditation garden. The small trees had new leaves, and the benches had been wiped clean, so why was I being led to the garden?

"Hey, Ms. D., look what I found," said Carlos as he held a baby bird. The other young men smiled and looked at me to see what I had to say.

"What happened?" I asked as I stepped closer. "The baby was just walking around in the garden with no mother," said Carlos. Practicing patience while waiting for me to help solve the problem, Carlos smiled and said, "Compassion for all life."

"Get a box with a top and line it with a towel so I can take it to a bird hospital in Lake Oswego," I said. They were on it. The bird would be saved. As I returned to the parking lot with the bird in a box, the young men returned to their living units for lunch.

During the twenty-five-mile drive to the bird hospital in Lake Oswego, the bird seemed happy, chirping during the entire trip. No one was in the waiting room when I arrived, so the little bird was seen immediately. A vet tech took the bird to the back and returned after a few minutes. "I gave him some fluids, but we just treat pet birds. I suggest you take the bird to the Audubon Society of Portland (now known as Bird Alliance of Oregon)," she recommended.

I got back in my SUV with the bird in a box to head north twenty-five more miles to get help. Road crews were doing repairs and detouring traffic along the winding road. The little bird chirped as I drove to my destination. I pulled up, looked for the entrance, and entered the foyer to wait for someone to help me. I noticed a large wooden box with a slot on the top for donations. I slipped a twenty-dollar bill inside and hoped I would soon hear some good news about the little bird—still chirping inside the box. A woman soon came to the counter and asked how she could help. "This little bird showed up in our meditation garden at the correctional site in Woodburn, and I wonder if you can help this baby bird," I said.

She asked to take the box with the bird inside to the back area. She wasn't gone long before returning to say, "This bird is nonnative to Oregon, so we can't take it." "What shall I do?" I asked. "Take it back where you found it, and the mother bird will return for her baby." Although I hoped to leave the bird, it was on its way back to the kennel. The little bird chirped all fifty return miles, and I thought to myself, *how do I tell a youth from Mexico that the bird is unwanted because it is not native to Oregon?*

When I slowly walked from the parking lot to the kennel, the youth were returning from lunch. They could see I still had the box and was carefully handling it. As I approached, the youth stopped. "Your little bird is named Chirpy," I announced with a smile. "What happened?" someone asked.

"The bird hospital only takes pet birds, so I took Chirpy to northwest Portland, where they rehabilitate birds. They don't take Chirpy's species," I continued. "They told me to bring him back where he was found, and his mother would find him."

The youth decided Carlos should oversee reuniting Chirpy with his mother. Carlos put Chirpy on the ground where he had been found and sat back under a tree, waiting for mom to show up. The other youth wanted to watch but thought having a bunch of human faces staring outside at Chirpy might scare the mom away. After a while, mom heard Chirpy's call and came to him. Carlos came inside smiling and told the others that the two birds were back together again. It had been an unusual day, but everyone seemed happy with the outcome for Chirpy.

FELIX GOES TO OREGON STATE PENITENTIARY

The usual afternoon routine tasks such as kennel cleaning, walking dogs, playing and training dogs, and bonding with the dogs were next on the day's agenda. While the youth were leashing their dogs for a walk around campus, I received a phone call from an administrator at the Oregon State Penitentiary (OSP) about adopting a dog. I had never been inside OSP, but

I agreed to get back to him. The administrator said, "The geese are pooping on the recreation yard. We need a dog to scare off the geese."

We were used to adopters coming to the kennel to determine which dog was the best fit for their living situation, but this would be a different adoption. This was the perfect opportunity to involve the youth in helping to determine if we had a dog that would be good at scaring the geese off the recreation yard. After returning from the afternoon dog walk, we started a conversation. I didn't expect a young man to say, "I don't like one of our dogs going to prison like us." I remained silent while everyone looked at me to say something. Finally, I said, "Well, let's talk about it." Another youth noted, "It doesn't seem right that we would be sending one of our dogs to prison." "Yeah, we want our dogs to live in a home with a family," was another comment.

I could feel the tension building as they continued talking with each other while they completed their assigned tasks at the kennel. "Let's talk about it more tomorrow. We don't have to decide right now," I said.

The next day, the young men came to me as a group with a plan they wanted me to consider. The spokesperson said, "We think it would be a good idea if you take Felix, but just for a visit. What if he is scared and doesn't want to be in prison?"

I could see where this was going, so I replied, "I like your idea of taking Felix for a visit since we do home visits with all our dogs to see if the place is appropriate. I will call OSP and let them know we want to visit before we make a final decision." Again, childhood memories surfaced about never having a say about what happened to the pets I loved. I was determined to strongly consider the feelings and thoughts coming from the young men.

Felix was a Munsterlander, a versatile hunting dog used for waterfowl. I set a date and time to bring Felix for a visit to the penitentiary. After checking in, I walked Felix down a hallway to the outside yard as "inmates" (now called "AICs" or "adults in custody") returned from the mess hall and went back to their cells. "Hey, look, a dog," an AIC yelled. Several men came to see Felix and wanted to interact with him. "It has been years since I have seen a dog," said one. How sad, I thought, but I was encouraged by how welcoming the AICs were when seeing a dog.

I left with Felix to talk to the young men about what I had observed, and they agreed to try it. The penitentiary adopted Felix in January 2011. The inmate chosen to be Felix's handler developed a bond very quickly. Felix had to stay in a guard's shed at night. The adoption was successful. Felix did his job of chasing the geese away from the recreation yard and was allowed to hang out in designated areas in the penitentiary.

I soon learned that Felix's handler received a negative health assessment—he had cancer and did not have long to live. Felix was allowed inside the infirmary and lay on the bed with his handler. Before Felix's handler passed, he designated another adult in custody, Steven, to care for this now beloved dog. Steven took to Felix immediately and was approved to build a shelter against a wall outside one of the buildings. When I visited, I looked at the shelter. Steven said, "Here in this cupboard is where I keep each meal for a week in sandwich bags should there be a lockdown and I cannot get food to Felix." He had a toothbrush, dog toothpaste for brushing Felix's teeth, and other needed supplies and supplements. There was a wading pool for summer and toys for Felix. This dog had become Steven's furry child.

Steven had a special area for Felix and provided a watermelon, toys, an outdoor swimming pool, and other items for mental stimulation. They bonded, and Felix was a comfort to the adults in custody during hospice or when interacting with a nonjudgmental dog. (Photo by Steven Johnston.)

Steven worked at the penitentiary and saved his earnings to pay for Felix's medical and other needs. Steven was extremely well organized. He kept all the veterinary records organized by year, and the infirmary nurses gave Felix needed shots (other than rabies).

The business of photographing Felix with the children of an AIC became immensely popular. Each photograph had a small charge, with the funds going to Felix's account. Steven had various costumes for Felix to wear to celebrate the yearly holidays. We often received letters and photos of Felix in which he is described as "My Pride and Joy." Steven's mental health professional, a licensed counselor, documented the changes Felix had made in Steven's mental health. He wrote,

I have observed your impressive behavioral change process and have noticed the positive influence that your role as caretaker for Felix has been on your personality and outlook towards life. You have demonstrated an enduring commitment to Felix in the past six years. You and Felix share a meaningful bond that is mutually beneficial, and I do not doubt that this will continue if you are given the opportunity.

NOTES FROM ADULTS IN CUSTODY

Steven asked those interacting regularly with Felix if they wanted to share what Felix meant to them. Some of the excerpts are as follows:

He allows men to show feelings and allows them to trust . . . there is nothing like unconditional love from a dog to warm your soul. CH

Not just a pooch, a valued member of our gated community . . . a four-legged hunk of love. FR

Felix does not care about race, ethnicity, or your charges. If you show him that you care and give him attention, he will return the favor! Felix brings hope, a sense of freedom, and comradery. JL

The first time I saw Felix, I could not help but smile. I always had dogs and missed the unconditional friendship. . . . No matter how bad a day one look at Felix lifts my mood. Being able to pet him is therapeutic. J.

He makes me feel the 'child heart' again . . . Thank you for the moments of comfort. S.S.

Felix is much more than a bird dog, he is our therapy dog, he is our friend, he is our family. Please continue your work. If it can affect men like my brother and me, you'll be giving hope to the next generation. Please encourage all to support rescue programs, especially in prisons. You'll be saving more than just dogs. JO

Steven advocated for taking Felix with him when he left corrections. He had $4,000 in an account to meet Felix's medical and other needs. However,

Steven was not encouraged to take Felix with him. I wrote to the administrator: "Steven and Felix have an extraordinarily strong bond, which is extremely important for mental health. I am willing to take Felix back to Project POOCH and keep him there until Steven has a job and a stable living situation. I can pick up Felix at your convenience." The letter did not go anywhere. I then contacted some people who knew the administrator to help release Felix. The administrator never responded. I'm still hoping Felix will be paroled since he's been incarcerated for twelve years. A man working in the penitentiary leather shop made a beautiful collar with Felix's name and GOV.PARDON. I still have the collar and hope Felix can wear it someday.

Steven was released without Felix, and said, "I don't understand why they won't release Felix. You even told them you would look for a younger POOCH dog to take Felix's place."

Steven was immediately employed by Dave's Killer Bread, a supporter of released inmates looking for living-wage jobs. Steven received a positive performance review. However, it became more challenging to work the night shift because of transportation issues. There were no open positions besides the night shift; Steven has moved on to employment as a highway flagger. He has already been promoted and is trusted to drive the company truck. He expressed hope that he could still get Felix released, so I decided to write Collette Peters, head of corrections, seeking her help in getting a "pardon" for Felix so he could be reunited with Steven. Although I sent the letter by certified mail with a required signature, the only proof of delivery was the green card from the postal service showing that her office had received it. Since Peters no longer works at the Oregon State Penitentiary, I recently sent a request to the current superintendent but have not received a response.

Felix remains at the penitentiary doing what he does best at thirteen years of age.

20

Never Give Up Hope

COLBY'S STORY

Colby was born in Portland, Oregon, to parents aged seventeen. His parents had dropped out of high school but wanted to improve their parenting skills. When Colby was four years old, his parents married. They divorced fourteen years later.

Although Colby was shy, he did fine in school and liked math. His first-grade teacher helped him and said she saw something in him. She cried when he moved on to second grade. Then his parents started moving to different places, which disrupted Colby's schooling. As he entered high school, he became tired of the constant arguing between his parents. He didn't want to be home, so he found older kids drinking and smoking marijuana to escape their difficulties.

Colby's dad would let him make his own choices but grounded him when he found out about the drugs. Colby was skipping school and erasing messages about not being in school on his parents' answering machine. "I was easily influenced and began getting into fights because I took drugs from others," said Colby. Curfew and minor-in-possession (MIP) violations started occurring. "I just couldn't stand being at home listening to my parents arguing," he said.

One evening, Colby went to a party and drank too much, so he walked home. As he and his friend walked by a car with some guys in it, they started bad-mouthing each other. His friend punched one of the guys in the car and took his cell phone. The victim gave chase. Colby soon discovered that his friend had a knife and had stabbed the guy he had stolen the cell phone from. Colby's friend ran off. The police showed up to find Colby standing at the site of the altercation. Colby explained to the police what had happened, but he wasn't allowed to plea, and his case went to trial. Colby was sentenced to seven years and would be released at age twenty-five.

When he arrived at the MacLaren Youth Correctional Facility, he was depressed for a year. He was required to participate in anger management classes and to think before acting. He graduated high school and began working in the campus canteen to make as much money as possible. He soon learned from other young men about working with dogs on campus. He admitted that he thought the dog handlers just walked dogs around campus, so he applied to be accepted into the program. Working with dogs requires an interview. Colby's peers made up most of the interview committee. Colby said, "I was nervous during the interview; it was only my second interview in my whole life. My other interview was with Subway, and only one person did the interviewing."

Colby was accepted into the program after being at MacLaren for a year. Colby was a lot happier working with dogs and a lot less depressed. He noted, "I had something to look forward to for the next six years, and the young men in the program were more mature. It was much better than sitting in my living unit. There are a lot of books to read at the kennel, and I liked that because it made me mad when I couldn't figure out what I needed to do to make an abused dog better." Colby looked at a dog like a math problem: Find the first step that works and then move on to the next, building a solid foundation. A typical problem: How do I get a dog to do something I want?

Colby's dog, Callie, came in with her own set of problems. Callie was not happy, and her hackles stood up straight. A few of the guys in the program walked away from her care, but Colby liked working with things to see if he could observe a change and help in some way. Callie was a big challenge, but Colby was willing to take on one. Callie would growl and bark at Colby, but he learned to gain her trust. She looked forward to Colby coming to the kennel daily to take her for walks, teach her new things, and hang out together. Colby would dress Callie in hats and coats for those cold, rainy mornings. He said, "I always wanted a sibling, but it just never happened. Growing up, there were dogs, and I would tell them my secrets. I told Callie my secrets and thoughts, too."

Colby got along with his fellow dog handlers and always learned new things. He listened to the dog trainer and practiced what she taught him. He would even go beyond the basic requirements and teach Callie tricks

Although Callie was in Project POOCH for seven years and she got along with the youths in the program, the potential adopters, not so much. She had been picked up by a county shelter and brought to Project POOCH in hopes a home could be found for her. It never happened until Joan, the executive director, brought her to her newly created dog sanctuary for dogs like Callie. (Photo from author's collection.)

like turning out the lights. He would bring peanut butter from his living unit to the kennel and put it on a light switch to teach Callie how to turn it off.

After working with the dogs for a while and showing great improvement in his ability to deal with his anger and think before acting, Colby was allowed to transfer across the state to a halfway house where he could work off-site for half a day and then return to the "camp building" in the evening. It was an opportunity to gradually learn how to acclimate to the outside world after being locked up for many years. Colby didn't jump at the opportunity because he now felt comfortable where he was and did not want to leave Callie. He talked to the kennel manager and others to make the right decision. Finally, he decided to stretch his ability to apply what he had learned and took the opportunity.

After leaving MacLaren, he second-guessed his decision but soon was able to leave the "camp" and work at the local humane society, where he started training the dogs so they would be more adoptable. After helping at the humane society for about a month, he emailed that there was a Border collie mix named Bullseye that he had been working with, and when he turned around to look at the dog as he was leaving for the day, the dog seemed to be saying, "Why are you leaving me?" Colby called me and asked if POOCH would take the dog into the program because no one seemed interested in adopting the dog.

I was very happy to learn of Colby's continuing interest in saving dogs and his reaching out to see if he could get help for Bullseye. I agreed to send my assistant halfway across the state to bring Bullseye to Project POOCH if someone from the shelter could travel with the dog over the mountains for a meet up.

Bullseye wasn't with us very long because an adopter came forward and renamed him Scooter. He brings a lot of joy to the woman adopter. The woman brings Scooter to the office from time to time so that we can see how happy he is and provide some opportunities for new photos to be shared with Colby. Since we had such good luck finding a home for Bullseye (aka Scooter), Colby asked about POOCH taking another dog. We also found a home for this dog after additional training at Project POOCH.

Colby continued working with other dogs at the shelter while still incarcerated. He was then moved to another "camp" on the Oregon coast. He was happy to learn that two dogs at this camp had come from a local humane society to be trained and adopted.

CALLIE'S FAILED ADOPTIONS

Callie, the first dog Colby worked with at MacLaren, still had not found a home. Colby thought about her and asked how she was doing. He wanted to know if she had had any home visits and how they went. Callie's first home visit was going great until a friend of the potential adopter arrived wearing a raincoat, a wide-brimmed canvas rain hat, and an umbrella by her side. As the friend started walking toward Callie in the back of my SUV with the hatch open, she growled and gave a menacing bark. I quickly closed the hatch of my SUV and decided not to push the visit in hopes she might calm down and be accepting of the friend. I thanked the potential adopter and her friend for the opportunity to see if Callie was the right dog for them.

Colby asked, "Will you talk to Susie, our dog trainer?"

I replied, "Yes, we need to find out how to correct her behavior."

We soon had another interested adopter. The potential adopter was an Oregon State Park ranger. The dog handlers hoped that Callie would score a win this time, but it was not to be. The applicant backed out before a visit could be done.

"Oh, this looks like a good application," I told the dog handlers a few days later. It was from a single mom with a teenage daughter living in southeast Portland. I was upbeat and asked the dog handlers to remember that it isn't about getting rid of a dog, it is about finding the right home for our dogs. When it was time for the visit, the youths helped me load up a crate, Callie's records, a booklet on dos and don'ts when adopting, food for a few days, and the blanket Callie had been sleeping on. I was on my way, with an estimated arrival time of 11 a.m. I felt so good about this visit and was talking to Callie on the way to her new adoptive home. I am not sure she heard what I said. She just loved riding in the SUV and happily settled in for the journey.

Upon arrival, I left Callie in my SUV while I checked out the fenced yard. The yard passed our requirements. I handed the mom and daughter some treats for Callie and told them I would acclimate her to their backyard before showing them Callie's commands. After Callie sniffed around the area, I handed the leash to the mom while I walked around the yard with them. The daughter beamed as she tried walking Callie. After forty-five minutes, I asked, "Would you like to do an overnight?" They were on board. I headed back to my car to get the crate for safety reasons should strangers arrive at the house overnight.

When I arrived back at the kennel, the young men were anxious to hear how Callie did on her visit. "She's on an overnight, and I'll call in the morning to find out if it was a success," I said. The following day, I got a call from the mom: "We put Callie in her crate for the night; however, when my daughter returned to the house late in the evening, Callie barked aggressively." I agreed to come to pick up Callie—a failed adoption. Euthanasia was never an option. We would keep trying.

I made an appointment for Callie to see an animal behaviorist for help. Susie, our dog trainer, agreed to go with me. We came away with several pages on how to work with Callie and medication for her anxiety. We soon had another potential adopter for Callie—a woman about thirty-five years old. She sat down on the sofa in our training area at the kennel. Two dog handlers brought out Callie's folder with information for the adopter to review. They told her about Callie and how she was wary of strangers but had seen a behaviorist, and we noted improvement.

Callie was behaving herself, so we relaxed. One of the dog handlers looked at the woman and said, "When Callie comes over to greet you, do not put your hand over her head." But the woman did just what he said not to do, and Callie bit her thumb, a drop of blood showing. One dog handler ran to get the emergency kit, and I used an alcohol wipe before putting a bandage on the woman's thumb. As I walked the woman from the kennel to the correctional facility's exit, she acted like the bite was no big deal. She was still interested in a home visit with Callie. A week later, I received a bill from her doctor.

CALLIE VISITS COLBY AT CAMP

Colby frequently contacted me, trying to find a way to solve Callie's problems so she could be adopted. He asked if I could bring Callie to visit him at the corrections camp on the Oregon coast. After clearing my visit with the staff, I took Callie to see Colby. They were overjoyed to see each other. Colby said, "I'm getting out soon. Do you think you could bring Callie to where I am staying?"

"Yes, we can arrange that as long as your landlord will allow Callie to come for a visit," I responded.

After Colby was released from corrections, I took Callie to visit him. However, Colby needed to get a job and settle before I could consider a permanent adoption for Callie. I explained my thoughts about him adopting Callie so soon. He agreed that he had to make a lot of decisions about his job and living situation before he adopted a dog.

By now, Callie had been in the program for seven years. She knew the kennel and the campus where she went on her daily walks. The dog handlers were always careful when introducing her to any new youths in the program. After so many years, she was comfortable in the kennel. However, I wasn't giving up on getting Callie into a forever home.

21

More Challenges

The young men and I were learning from each other, and the dogs were often our teachers. We collaborated with dog experts on turning unwanted behavior into desirable behavior—much like the young men were learning in their treatment classes led by corrections counselors and mental health professionals. I doubt any of us realized how difficult it could be to change some undesirable behaviors due to past trauma.

REDD GOES TO RESCUE IN WASHINGTON

Redd, a sixty-pound cattle dog mix, had been in the kennel way too long, but putting a dog down because of no adopter was not an option. We were going to look at other options for Redd. I tried a local rescue and offered to return Redd to us if he was not a good fit. The response was a flat-out no. I tried, "Well, how about a trade where your rescue takes Redd, and we take one of your dogs already in rescue?" Not interested.

A friend had seen a website of a rescue in the state of Washington that would pick up hard-to-place dogs from shelters throughout the United States. We weren't interested in having someone come to us and take Redd. We wanted to know where he would be going and see the place in person. The website was attractive, and we agreed to the four-hour drive. The rescue manager said he would stay in touch during the drive and help us find the place if needed.

We had purchased a large enclosure for the rescue to put Redd in because they were short of space. It had been delivered, so we loaded up other belongings for Redd and headed north early in the morning. Tracy Lucas and Mark Oronzo (Ginger's adopters and longtime volunteers for Project POOCH) were happy to ride along. Tracy had bonded with Redd and wanted to be sure it was a proper placement. On the way north, we made a pact—if this rescue were not suitable for Redd, we would not leave him.

The rescue manager called. "Where are you guys?" I answered, "About an hour away is my best guess." Upon arriving at the small town where the rescue was located, we stopped at a bar to ask for directions. We were almost there, according to the server. We called the rescue manager to say we would arrive in about ten minutes. We found the place and pulled into a parking spot. We stared at a massive mountain of waste from the kennel area. The manager escorted us to a side area of the building, which appeared to be a Quonset hut. We had to dodge dog feces that had not been picked up as we walked, but we said nothing to the manager. "I would like to see where you put the enclosure I sent for Redd," I said. We followed the manager to an unfinished area with a cement mixer and other storage items. It reminded me of what inmates hate—being put in the hole with no outside contact. "May we see the other dogs you have here?" I asked. "Oh, no. They are all eating," was the reply.

I was starting to see some red flags about the place. Tracy said she was going to the vehicle to see how Redd was doing. Since the manager wasn't willing to take us on a tour of his facility, we went back to the side yard so he could bring out a dog. He brought out a small pug mix he had picked up from another rescue in the United States.

I was in a quandary, wondering how we could get out of this situation. I announced, "I am going to check on Tracy and Redd." I found Tracy in the cargo area of my vehicle, where she was consoling Redd. She had somehow become locked in the cargo area with Redd and couldn't unlock the hatch. With the touch of a button, she was freed from her predicament.

"Tracy, I know you'll agree we aren't leaving Redd here," I told her. "There are too many red flags. You stay here, and I'll go back inside and tell the manager you're upset about leaving Redd, and we're taking him back to Project POOCH." Smiling through her tears, she nodded her head yes. It was time to get out of the place. I told the manager, "Tracy is too bonded with Redd, and we are taking him back with us." Mark didn't say much, but I knew he agreed by his facial expressions. Once we were back in the vehicle, I contacted the kennel to let them know that Redd was coming back. I could hear the young men shout joyfully.

Since it was a long trip, we found a dog-friendly motel with an adjoining restaurant where we toasted with glasses of water and said, "We did the right thing." Not long after, we learned that volunteers at the rescue in Washington had videotaped the deplorable conditions inside the rescue.

Other rescues wanted their dogs back, so some dogs were put in a long-haul truck and headed to a rescue in another state. Some never made it.

When we arrived back at Project POOCH the next day, I explained to the young men why we didn't leave Redd. I noted, "That's why we do home visits for our dogs, and that's why you always check out a child daycare before you leave your child there while you go to work."

RIP REDD

Redd continued living at Project POOCH, where he was loved and cared for by the young men. Unfortunately, Redd developed cancer, and our veterinarian told us he did not have much longer. I discussed the prognosis with the young men and Tracy. Being open with them was important. Their feelings need to be respected. Tracy asked to be with Redd on the day of the final goodbye. She and I would comfort him as the veterinarian humanely euthanized him. I had taken Redd from the kennel to the veterinary clinic and waited for Tracy to arrive. When she entered the room, she had a burger to feed Redd, a special last meal.

Redd was diagnosed with advanced cancer and enjoyed a treat with his favorite volunteer before his final goodbye. (Photo from author's collection.)

Redd was cremated, and we had a ceremony in the meditation garden where he liked to hang out with the young men. We placed his ashes in the garden. After Redd's ceremony, a young man told me that he felt sad for Redd because he had never experienced life away from the kennel with a family. He was loved at the kennel, but it would have been great for him to experience life away from there. Years later, a young man who had been Redd's handler called me to say, "When I got out of MacLaren, I had dreams about Redd. He was a good dog."

22

Keeping Hope Alive

We usually had shelters asking us to come and rescue large dogs; however, a call came regarding a nineteen-pound dog named Gizmo. He was thought to be a Jack Russell mixed with a terrier. He had fleas, matted fur, and a lot of hair loss on his back and buttocks. Our volunteer dog temperament tester passed him up on her first visit because she was looking for a different dog; however, Gizmo was still there when she returned three weeks later. Since the shelter had a limited budget, Gizmo did not receive medical care or full flea control. He did get a flea bath because the workers did not want to handle a dog full of fleas.

GIZMO COMES TO POOCH

Our tester assessed Gizmo after he had been at the shelter for a month. His chart read "unknown" regarding children, other dogs, and food/toy aggression. He was a dog with no history. He was active and allowed the tester to pick him up. He was more interested in his environment and sniffed around a lot. After a while, he was tested with a pug in the shelter and did fine. Gizmo needed the help of Project POOCH, but our tester was worried about the expense of vaccinations, worming, flea treatment, and tests for the reason behind his hair loss. He was neutered, so that was a good thing. Before going to an adoptive home, he was going to Project POOCH for good health and basic training.

Since the program began, Dr. Debbie Unrau had given complimentary vaccinations to POOCH dogs. She also came monthly to talk with the young men about best practices for dogs. She discussed Gizmo's health situation with the dog handlers. Richard, a Project POOCH dog handler, became Gizmo's caretaker. It was love at first sight. Richard gave Gizmo a bath, flea treatment, and an identification tag. When Dr. Unrau examined Gizmo, she thought he was about four years old, so Richard gave Gizmo a birthdate of September 25, 2008.

Winter soon came, and Richard asked if he could get Gizmo a warm coat for dog walks. Our local pet store had one on sale that was a perfect fit. Gizmo seemed to know he was now getting royal treatment. He proved to be very smart and motivated to learn good doggy manners. He became a star at agility and entertained visitors to the program. After Gizmo passed his Canine Good Citizen test, we received an application from a couple with no children in the home. But they had a cat.

WHO WILL ADOPT GIZMO?

Denise Mason, a volunteer, said she would drive 170 miles north with Gizmo in hopes he would find the right home. On the home visit, Gizmo seemed to fit in and was mildly curious about the family cat. Denise spent an hour reviewing Gizmo's medical and behavior file, and showing the adoptive parents his training cues. She then headed back to the correctional facility. After driving more than halfway back, she received a call from the adopters: "Gizmo went after the cat, but we will crate him overnight and meet you halfway tomorrow to return him." The adopters cried as they handed Gizmo over with his bed and toys. That was home visit number one.

Home visit number two was a local family interested in a companion for their other small dog. On the day of the visit, Gizmo strutted in like he owned the place. He started his entertainment act by playing with balls and other antics. His intensity in pursuing balls was relentless. Gizmo spent the night and even slept in the parents' bed with them and their other little dog, but their eight-year-old daughter was afraid of Gizmo. The "real" Gizmo surfaced. He did not want to share the family, toys, or food with the other dog. He came back to Project POOCH.

It was beginning to look like stories of foster children who move from foster home to foster home, never finding a home where they could live permanently. I could tell the young men felt hopeless about Gizmo finding a home; however, I reminded them that we never give up—some dogs take longer than others.

Richard was getting attached to Gizmo by now and could often be observed holding him, much as a person would do with an infant child. I thought, *if dogs can teach young male offenders how to treat children by working with dogs, that would be good.*

"Don't give up," said another young man to Richard after the multiple adoptions failed. By now, Richard didn't care if Gizmo got adopted because he had enjoyed having the little dog to care for and teach tricks to since the Canine Good Citizen test had been passed months ago.

Home visit number three was coming up, and the adopters had had a Jack Russell die recently. They had two other dogs—both over one hundred pounds. Gizmo did fine until Denise left him for the night. He settled in quickly and decided he would take on the big dogs, and they absolutely could not have their toys. He even went after the big dogs for coming near a toy. Once again, he went to sleep with the family for one night only. Tears flowed, but everyone knew it wasn't the right home for Gizmo.

A young man called, saying he was living with his mother. They had no other pets, so we hoped home visit number four would work. The young man thought Gizmo was perfect until he experienced the dog's energy level. He decided to give Gizmo back to Project POOCH, which upset his mother so much that she left for the day because she couldn't bear to witness Gizmo leaving. The Project POOCH staff and dog handlers analyzed Gizmo's home visit failures and decided to develop a case management plan outlining what home would be an appropriate forever home for Gizmo. We all agreed that having four failed home visits gave us valuable information in finding placement for Gizmo.

GIZMO WINS THE LOTTERY

While working with a trainer, Erin, at a local gym, I shared Gizmo's story. She said, "I run up to twenty-five miles a day and think Gizmo might be the ideal dog to run with." However, her husband was interested in a big dog, like a Labrador retriever. They visited our available dogs for adoption and decided Gizmo would join their family. After learning about all of Gizmo's past adoption failures, they wanted to talk it over and get back to us. They read books and asked many questions to ensure they would be excellent dog parents. Home visit number five could not have been more perfect for Gizmo. He got lots of exercise and was the only pet. They kept up on his training and felt they had won the lottery with Gizmo.

I cannot say that Richard was happy about the adoption, but he understood that he needed to let go so that Gizmo could finally get the life he deserved. After adopting Gizmo, Erin always had entertaining stories to tell me when I saw her at the gym. Sometime after the adoption, Erin informed me that she and her husband were divorcing. She assured me not to worry about Gizmo because she would have sole custody. "I will never give him up. He's in his forever home," she emphasized. I let my breath out with a sigh of relief.

One day, Erin told me she had met someone and would be moving to Europe. She had secured housing where she could have Gizmo. They would be living in Belgium. She often sent me photos of Gizmo exploring his new surroundings. She said, "I never would have left Oregon without him." Although Gizmo has passed away, she keeps his toys where he left them. "Gizmo changed my life for the better. He lives on in my heart," she said.

23

Letting Go Is Never Easy

Over almost three decades, Project POOCH had grown from a kennel with two dogs to an organization able to house seventeen dogs. We were doing increasingly more fundraising events and a yearly gala where the former POOCH participants spoke to a crowd of friends and donors.

WHEN IT'S TIME TO LEAVE

As executive director, it took me a while to realize it was time to find someone else to take over the program. I soon realized it was not going to be easy. While several people appeared right for the position, grasping the program meant wearing many hats—especially the corrections piece. Where would we find someone passionate about incarcerated teens and shelter dogs? The person would also need the ability to raise funds, understand financial statements, and engage with donors, volunteers, and corrections staff.

In 2019, at the end of the yearly gala event, I announced I would leave the organization. Former youths were at the event and showed appreciation for me and the program that improved their lives. Anthony, the first youth, attended with his wife. He gave me the award that I have placed in my home office, along with group photos of the many youths in the program over the years.

THREE LONG-TERM DOGS AT THE KENNEL

My exit from Project POOCH meant leaving three hard-to-place dogs for someone else to deal with; however, I could not walk away from these dogs as my father had done with my childhood pets. I had looked for a few years, knowing I could not live with myself if I did not try to find a place where the three dogs (Callie, Kiera, and River) could live their lives. It was a good lesson in patience for the young men and the importance of never giving up hope on your dream. It may take longer than one would hope.

DONORS APPEAR

As happened in 1993, when I started Project POOCH, donors stepped forward and wanted to help me with the next phase of my dream. With $10,000 from Dolores Smith and her husband Lloyd Wood, $10,000 from my savings, and $10,000 from Tracy Lucas, I had enough for fencing on one acre in the country where my home was located. I also purchased individual dog sleeping areas with igloos to keep them warm during cold weather. The property had a big, heated outbuilding for housing the dogs. A donor stepped forward, and I was able to move the three dogs to this new forever home. Yes, people care enough to invest in the future of incarcerated teens and homeless dogs. I have always been grateful for the support I needed to provide a forever home for Kiera, Callie, and River.

Kiera was the first dog to leave the kennel environment and move to my newly formed nonprofit, R and K Sanctuary for Dogs. At one year old, she was surrendered to the Willamette Humane Society in Salem, Oregon. Along with her littermate, she had been an outside dog. Both were malnourished. She was listed as a Labrador/mastiff and had not been spayed. One of our volunteers had passed on her; however, I traveled to the shelter to check her out. She was not considered a beautiful or cute dog, but I liked how friendly she was, so I took her to Project POOCH. She bonded with volunteers and the dog handlers, but her several home visits were unsuccessful. We got input from our dog trainer on making Kiera, a fifty-eight-pound dog, an adoptable dog.

One afternoon, our regular staff was out, and there was a substitute Kiera liked, so they went on a walk with the other dogs and their handlers. While on the walk, another staff member stopped to show the substitute her new tattoo on her ankle. As soon as the staff person lifted her ankle, Kiera bit her. The staff said, "I am going to have to take time off and go to the doctor because I have MRSA." *Oh, great,* I thought. POOCH ended up paying for her time off from work and the cost of the doctor's visit.

Volunteer Tracy Lucas and I made an appointment to take Kiera to the Animal Behavior Clinic for an assessment. The diagnosis was fear-related aggression/territorial aggression. The treatment plan was too much for adopters. They wanted a dog that would not be a lot of work, and a possible biter that could bring lawsuits. I talked with the young men about the assessment, and they wanted to keep trying to help get her adopted. They also knew that sometimes the shelters do not get the correct breeds on mixes, so we sent a mouth swab to the Wisdom Panel. She returned as a Labrador retriever, boxer, collie, and Siberian husky mix. Sean, a youth in the program, then said, "Now we have accurate breed information. Let's make a new flyer and post new information on our website and Petfinder. Seeing the young men interested in solving a problem was gratifying.

I took Kiera on a couple more home visits but did not leave her due to her fear. I decided to move her to the sanctuary. The "K" in the sanctuary stands for her name. She had the best room at the sanctuary because she could stay in the sunroom while the other two dogs stayed in the heated shop at night. I had areas for three dogs in the shop, but Kiera and Callie didn't get along, so I separated them to avoid a serious dogfight.

In January 2020, I was at a late starting meeting, which irritated me, but I decided to have a cheerful outlook and not show agitation. At 1:00 p.m., the meeting was in full swing after everyone had introduced themselves and shared something about abundance in their lives. Everyone was making statements such as "I feel abundance just being in this room" or "I feel abundance being around such caring people." When it came to my turn, I said, "I feel abundance for the homeless dogs in my care." Some laughed, and others turned to see who was making such a statement. At 1:30 p.m., I felt compelled to quietly leave the meeting by tiptoeing through the kitchen and down the hallway to the exit. Soon, I was at the sanctuary.

Fifteen-year-old Kiera was waiting to be released from the sunroom and into a side yard to relieve herself. After I let her out, I went to the shop to release the other two dogs (River and Callie) into a separate yard. I pulled River out of the yard with Callie and took him to Kiera's yard for playtime. River went up and smelled Kiera's rear end, which got her attention. She responded by doing a slow run due to arthritis in her rear legs. After about five minutes of playtime, I moved River back to his area with Callie and prepared a meal for them.

It was a clear day outside (no rain, which is unusual this time of year), so I left Kiera in the yard while I cleaned the floor in the sunroom, where she had an accident while I was gone. After about fifteen minutes, I looked in the yard and saw Kiera had collapsed. I hurried outside and tried to pull her up, but she cried in pain and was dead weight. I ran to get a device made especially for dogs with difficulty using their back legs. I could get it under her but could not lift it. She was struggling to breathe, and her eyes were losing their life.

Former board member Pamela Owen lived about a half hour away and was always an expert at helping me catch loose dogs. She had strong arms from kayaking, so I called her as I was in tears. "Kiera collapsed, and I can't pick her up," I cried. "I think she's going into shock, and I need to take her to the Emergency Veterinary Clinic of Tualatin."

I kept running back to Kiera, begging her not to die. I pulled my SUV around to the back of the house so it would be easier to get Kiera from the fenced area and loaded. I called the ER in advance to be prepared for our arrival and checked to see if Pamela had arrived. I locked the house and was ready to go once we loaded Kiera. Pamela picked up Kiera and got her safely in the back of my open SUV.

KIERA GOES TO THE EMERGENCY CLINIC

Luckily, there was little traffic Sunday afternoon, so we arrived at the emergency clinic within thirty minutes. The place was packed with cats in carriers and small dogs held by their owners, and everyone had a bag of popcorn to munch on while waiting their turn for a doctor to see their beloved pet. I told the receptionist I had called in, and my dog was in shock. "Could someone please come out with a stretcher?" I asked in desperation. After collecting fees from someone on the way out, she said, "We are very busy tonight. We will get to you when we can."

I took a deep breath and stood in the middle of the waiting area since all the chairs were taken. I didn't want Kiera to die in the back of my SUV without me by her side, but I had no other choice than to wait for someone to come with a stretcher. Two young medical assistants finally showed up with a stretcher and followed me outside to transfer Kiera, bring her around the building, and take her into the hospital. Pamela and I found a couple of chairs in the lobby and waited until someone had some news about Kiera's condition.

The young woman on her cell phone waited with her cat in a carrier. She was escorted to a back room where pet owners could say goodbye to their beloved pets.

A Boston terrier showed up wearing purple bandages around his two front legs. His family pulled him up on a sofa, letting him cuddle between them. The woman in the family was unaware that the Boston terrier hoped she would drop one of the Cheetos she was eating. None fell.

A tall man with an empty water bottle was called to a room. After a while, he came out while medical personnel took his little tan Chihuahua with a gray muzzle back to the surgery room. The man never looked back as his little dog watched him leave.

Finally, a doctor came over to talk to me about Kiera. There was no broken leg, but the doctor had given her oxygen because her gums were a muddy color. When they took her off oxygen, she gasped for air and was having great difficulty breathing. He said, "There is no hope. We have seen old dogs like her with the same problem, and they never survived."

"So, it is just better to let her pass?" I asked. He nodded yes. He went on to say that if I wanted to be with her as she passed, he would let me know when the room was available. Once I decided to be with her when she passed, the receptionist called me to fill out the paperwork and provide a credit card. A big sign read: NO CHECKS.

When the doctor came to the waiting room with Kiera on a stretcher and a dark gray blanket covering her body, Pamela and I went together to the room where we would say our final goodbyes. Kiera was alert enough to know that it was me who was holding her paw and head as I told her what a good dog she had been and how much I loved her. Pamela gently massaged the exposed side of her body. There was a buzzer to be pushed when I felt it was time for the doctor to administer the end-of-life medication. Her body did not move as the medication was administered. Her heart and lungs were rapidly losing their ability to keep her alive. She was cremated, and her ashes were given to her former handler at his request.

I texted her former youth POOCH handler, who had been out of the correctional facility for ten years. He expressed sadness but was happy that she had not been alone. We talked about the memories she had left us. We had tried several adoptions, but Kiera didn't like cats, little kids, or men with hats. When I realized the kennel environment was not a good option for her anymore, I knew it was time for her to come into my life full-time. She had a good appetite the day she passed; she was interested in playing with River, so it was unexpected that suddenly she would collapse. At least her suffering was not long-term.

All the young men and I have worked with experienced much happiness when working with the dogs. But we were never prepared for how hard it would be to let go of a beloved companion. Andrew composed a poem in Kiera's honor:

In loving memory
of a Faithful friend
and Companion.
Her energy, loyalty,
and love of life
will be missed.

24

In Their Own Words

Occasionally, I sought feedback from the young men about their experiences in Project POOCH. If I expected them to show improvement, I needed to hear their perspective on the program. The youth not only learned about dogs. They learned how to work with others, how to ask for help, and how to communicate with adopters and guests. It was very satisfying to them when they realized that they had learned about themselves and how they could do better. A sampling of their thoughts, ideas, and experiences follows.

PERSONAL CHANGES I'VE UNDERGONE

> *During my time at Project POOCH, I took the opportunity to improve my character in various ways. I learned much about work ethics and what it means to follow a specific work schedule. I gained better manners, became more social, and trained thirteen dogs, which helped me gain a sense of responsibility and patience.*
>
> *At age twenty-two, Project POOCH was the first workplace I have ever been employed at. Before I became incarcerated, I was so nervous and lacked so much discipline that I never even tried filling out an application for a job. When I received the job, I knew it was time to learn how to be consistent and reliable and communicate professionally with people. Working at Project POOCH made me understand that we should always be aware of how we can improve ourselves.*
>
> *The best thing about working at POOCH was the opportunity to interact with dogs, volunteers, and adopters.*
>
> *Our director did a very good job encouraging us to interact appropriately and politely with others. This helped us build a bigger sense of community and belonging and not feel so detached from other people. Many of us were so comfortable hanging out with our "friends" that we were too nervous, unsociable, and/or improper to become interested in*

communicating with people outside our regular group. Gaining social skills helped us become more professional when interacting with other people and have the confidence to speak in different settings.

LEARNING DOG TRAINING

Through all the dogs I have trained, I learned things more important to me than the dog training methods. The most important thing was to be more patient. When training a dog and they don't understand the method, I should never justify getting upset and impatient. The problem might be my way of teaching and not the dog's ability. I learned to watch others succeed with their dogs, which helped me develop alternative training methods for dogs in my care.

Project POOCH was a life-changing experience. It enriched my character with experiences and skills I will find useful for the rest of my life.

BAILEY THE DEAF DOG

In 2007, Colby was assigned to Bailey, a deaf Border collie. Here is his story in his own words.

I was told Bailey wasn't aggressive one bit. He is thirteen months old and has A LOT of energy. He was a stray with a chain choke collar embedded in his neck. After the vet removed the collar, I could see a very bad wound. It also smelled bad. Bailey is very sensitive and will nip at you if you try to touch his neck. We put some bathless leave-on shampoo on it, and Bailey tried to bite all four of us. He looks pretty playful with other dogs, but I don't want to try it until he is healed. The vet also neutered him, so I won't be able to bathe him for two weeks. I think he will hate the bath. I'll probably get bit. He bit Andrew today on the ankle. This dog will be very challenging, but I'll do whatever it takes to make him adoptable.

I walked Bailey this afternoon, and he walks very well when not around other dogs.

I worked on his sit, down, and stay. He is a very smart, food-motivated dog. Andrew is reliable and will work with Bailey when I am not at the kennel. I spent all day with him, both outside and inside. He is doing better with being touched. Still, if you touch close to the raw part of his neck, he will nip. He has very sharp teeth but when he bites, he doesn't come close to breaking skin so he is just letting me know not to touch him on his neck.

Bailey returned to the vet for a couple of days to have his neck checked. All the hair around his neck is shaved, and the raw part is healing. He seems to be more comfortable with his neck being touched.

He was in the yard on a leash, and there were five other dogs out (on leashes), and he lunged at them. The leash got tangled up under his leg, and when I went to fix it, he nipped at both me and the leash. He bruised my skin through my sweatshirt, but he could have done a lot more damage with his sharp teeth. He also tried to nip at me when I took his leash off him. Besides biting me several times, he's a good dog with lots of potential.

Bailey didn't nip at me today. He is a very smart dog. He is very playful. He is a good dog but has only been here four days, so he is still very stressed and apprehensive.

Bailey turned out to be very adoptable after consistency and trust were brought about through his training. Coincidentally, he alerted the woman adopter by jumping on her breast. A lump had formed, and she went to her doctor and was diagnosed with breast cancer.

DOGS HELPED ME TO CARE FOR OTHERS AND MY SURROUNDINGS

Working with shelter dogs has helped me with compassion and caring for others and my surroundings. The dogs helped me be more aware of my emotions. I now know that I have more feelings than just anger or being fine. Now, it's okay to shed tears from time to time.

I've learned a lot about handling dogs during grooming, obedience training, and general knowledge of dogs. We take care of basic maintenance needs at the kennel and have even remodeled the older kennel runs.

Project POOCH has also helped me with my social skills in dealing with people from the public and having conversations with our volunteers. It has helped me be the person I am today. Without POOCH, I don't think I could've ever become the respectable, mature individual I am today. I am forever grateful to be part of POOCH and how it has helped me as a human being.

A DOG'S OPTIMISM IS CONTAGIOUS

I have been in Project POOCH for two years. All dogs I have met resonate with me in some way or another. However, the common thing they share is how they teach me a little about myself and life in general. My hopes are in return, I can teach them love and trust and help them learn about themselves and life as it should be.

One example that sticks out in my head is Harley. Harley was in the program for quite some time. Many were convinced that Harley would be here for the long run. One day, we were proved wrong when Harley never returned from a home visit. What Harley taught me was hope. Always have hope, and things will work out for the best, sometimes when we least expect it.

Another example is Kiera. Kiera came from a terrible situation before she came to POOCH. However, she does not let her past define her, as she has learned to open up to the people who matter most to her. Although her love is not given to everybody, she is warming up gradually. Through Kiera, I have learned that sometimes our past situations weren't great, but perseverance is the key to overcoming such a thing.

I have learned from these wonderful four-legged companions. Their optimism is contagious to my well-being, and their mysterious work has taught me so much.

WHAT I LEARNED ABOUT PATIENCE

I learned about patience when I became a mentor at Project POOCH. I had to be patient when training a new person who entered the program. When a new person asks me more than once how to do something, it can be frustrating because I have already explained it several times. I take a deep breath and calm myself down. I then must learn the way a person learns best. This requires a lot of patience. I learned from working with the dogs that they don't always get the command I am trying to teach on the first or second try.

POOCH requires patience. It is a job where dog training is all about repetition and patience. There was one dog that was always working my patience. Her name was Lucy. Lucy was a three-year-old terrier mix. She came to us with no training. This was back in 2017, and I had just started working in the program. It took Lucy and me a couple of weeks to set up a "line of communication." In other words, she was very, and I mean VERY stubborn. She was also a very mischievous little dog. One day, she had an accident in her kennel run, and I had to put her in the front yard outside cages to clean her inside run. Keep in mind that the outside cage was made of chain link fencing. Unbeknownst to me, while I was cleaning the inside run, Lucy escaped from the cage through a small gap between the cage door and frame. I walked outside to check on Lucy and found her running around the front yard, acting goofy and celebrating her successful escape. I caught Lucy and put her in a different cage in the front yard. It was the exact same model.

I went back to doing what I had started earlier—cleaning Lucy's run. When I finished, I went to grab Lucy to put her back in her run. Again, unbeknownst to me, Lucy had also attempted to escape from this cage. She was unsuccessful this time. She probably thought, hey, I escaped from the same kind of cage once; I can escape from this one, too! It didn't work because zip ties secured this cage all around.

As I came out to get her, I noticed Lucy's head was stuck between the chain link fence and a zip tie with the gap secured. I ran fast to see what the situation was. Once I got there, I saw she tried to find her way out but got stuck. In doing so, the fence started choking her. Lucy was having trouble breathing. I grabbed the fence section and tried to lift it as much as possible to give her enough space to breathe, but I couldn't get her unstuck. I needed scissors to cut the zip tie. I couldn't just leave her there, so I started calling for the guys to help. They were out in the back area behind the building and couldn't hear my calls for help. I wasn't panicking. I was calm, collected, and was actively using patience. I would have stayed there all day until someone came out if needed. Luckily, one of the facility work crew was driving by, and I flagged him down. I asked him to call the POOCH staff on the radio. Help was on the way.

Patience is my ability to keep calm under stressful and pressing situations. I have learned how far my patience goes and how much further it can be pressed before it becomes too much. I show patience by always returning to my dogs after a short break if or when they stress me out too much. I had a chance to give up on a stressful situation with my dog but decided not to because I already had put a lot of my time, effort, and patience into my dog. Patience is key to training any dog to be successful.

Since I've been with the POOCH program, I've learned how patience can benefit my abilities as a dog handler. Through my prison sentence, I've come across difficult situations. It could be a staff member who has said something I didn't like or a youth testing me. I've made decisions based on the moment without thinking and not showing patience.

New dogs are always nerve-racking because I know little about dog handling. I'm still learning the ropes, so patience is crucial to success. I am working on being comfortable asking for help and listening to people speak to gain as much knowledge as possible. I appreciate Ms. D's and the staff's patience as I continue to grow and learn.

POOCH holds youth to a high standard. It will become part of me if I follow it and practice patience. I have learned that everyone works differently, every dog acts differently, and I must be patient to move forward with my life.

Since I started working at Project POOCH, I would say that the patience I have already acquired throughout my life has been thoroughly tested by these pups' many personalities.

Someone who has tested me daily and taught me so much about myself would be the dog Buckley. This dog has blessed me with the ability to have patience, understanding, and compassion. Buckley's condition requires me to prepare his special food, feed him countless times a day in a particular position so he doesn't regurgitate his food, and massage his throat daily to ensure he can eat and maintain a healthy weight.

This is time-consuming, messy, not the best smell, tedious, and repetitive. I'm okay with it because I see him healthy and full; he has progressed since being cared for by me. Because I was patient with him, I got to see the result of a happy and healthy dog who was full of life and just needed a little patience.

POOCH has taught me a lot about patience in my living unit, being incarcerated, and being a father, son, brother, and partner. Life will always test your patience, and you will always learn a new way to become patient. It's not easy, but there is a better payout if you wait, work hard, and listen. Patience will come.

I have shown compassion by meeting the needs of Buckley and other dogs craving attention and care. Buckley took a while to warm up to me, but he learned I was there to help him, not hurt him. The reason I didn't give up on Buckley is that I could relate to starvation, trust issues, and being under-socialized. Seeing me in him helped me have compassion for Buckley.

All he needed was someone to believe in him and not give up. Now Buckley is gone with his new family, happy and healthy. Because I showed him some compassion, I got the satisfaction of knowing that he would go on to have a great life. Seeing the outcome for a dog that was predetermined at birth to be unsuccessful and has the best possible outcome is the most gratifying feeling. This experience has left me wanting to be more compassionate to hopefully see more happy endings.

COMPASSION

Throughout my time here at POOCH, I've had the chance to dig deep into who I am as a person, and I wouldn't have been able to do that without the opportunity to work with these dogs.

A person can put up many barriers to protect oneself in this place we call home, but those barriers will break as soon as you take one look into a pup's face. Or a perfect sit from a big German shepherd that leans his head on your thigh to be petted and loved unconditionally.

Compassion works both ways between humans and animals. Dogs will love you more than anyone can and more than you could ever show yourself. I never liked to work with people. I'm more of an independent person, but working down here at the kennel, I've come to love the people I work with. I used to favor certain people over others, the same with dogs I would see growing up. One dog looks nicer than another, so the instinct is to flock to that dog. It's the same with people. Everyone goes at it at some point in their life.

When I work seven days a week with dogs from all over the state that have been through the trenches and back, the mindset of favoring starts to disappear, and I begin to see every dog as a living being that deserves love and compassion. Slowing that mindset became a part of me, and I continue to show it to the people I meet every day.

I don't know what it's like to be in another person's shoes or the mind of dogs that have spent years in a shelter; all I know is that compassion can create unbreakable bonds and heal damaged goods. The dogs have shown me that.

We took our dogs, Annie and Sophia, down to the Rockaway living unit to visit the youths. The guys were surprised to see the dogs as they were having lunch. The guys wanted to interact with the dogs. The dogs were as happy as ever, tails wagging, very excited to have people to play with them. Some guys were coming up to respectfully ask to pet Annie and ask if she knew any tricks. I showed them what she could do, and they were in awe. It was great to give the guys on Rockaway a chance to experience something different. Routines can become dreadful in a correctional setting. It's good to have dogs come over to play with the guys.

Two weeks later, Makai (our kennel supervisor) and my dog Annie visited Rockaway living unit on our second visit. One of the guys from the first visit had expressed that he was afraid of dogs because he had a terrible experience in his past. I encouraged him, along with his peers, to pet Annie. He had a big smile after he was able to overcome his fear of Annie.

We have had several Border collies in the program because people don't understand their energy level and that they are a working breed. A couple, Laurie and Colin came to look at one the veterinarian had told them about, but the dog already had an application.

Ms. Dalton said she knew of another Border collie at a local shelter that she could test if Laurie and Colin were willing to wait. They said they were willing to wait because they knew the breed and could provide the exercise needed.

The next day, Ms. Dalton went to the shelter, but their dog behaviorist said she thought the dog should be "put down." Well, Ms. Dalton brought the dog, Pete, to the program, and he has turned out to be the perfect dog for Laurie and Colin. Colin takes Pete to agility classes every week, and they have a dog walker for him too.

25

I Am Out! Now What?

Every incarcerated young man looks forward to the day of release from corrections. However, they often learn that finding an apartment, getting a job, and handling their finances is difficult. Here is what one former incarcerated young man said he encountered after being released from corrections.

> *When I was first released, I was very apprehensive. It seemed like a dream. I didn't know what to do. All I knew for sure was that I needed to start working and move to Portland, where I could be closer to the university. Those were my goals. I figured things couldn't be too hard. You can never prepare yourself for the types of obstacles and even peer pressure you may face when you get out. But optimism is key.*
>
> *I met my P.O. (parole officer) a week after I got out. She was rude to me and didn't provide any advice or assistance. I asked if I could move to Portland by March to be closer to the school. She said, "No." I asked for help finding apartments for felons. She said she didn't know. I was a little frustrated, but my new goal was to prove to her that I wasn't like most other people she deals with.*
>
> *I started working for Project POOCH in the community outreach office a week after I was released. It was nice to see how the organization works outside of corrections. I have learned many new skills since I started as their office assistant, and I am grateful for the opportunity.*
>
> *During my first month out, I was job searching every day. I applied for at least eight to ten jobs in about fifteen days. I also ran into some old friends. They really wanted me to go hang out, but I told them I was too focused on my future and couldn't let anything distract me.*
>
> *Some laughed at me, and some respected what I had said. These people weren't there for me while I was incarcerated for 7½ years, so why would I waste my time with them now?*

I interviewed at Petco, a dog training place. The Petco interview was the first time I had to explain my felony in person. I basically told him the short version, and I made that mistake when I was 17. I let him know that I did everything possible to change my life. Unfortunately, I didn't get the job. I was a little upset, but I knew I needed to stay positive and keep moving forward. Luckily, I got a job at a doggy daycare. It is a nice place, and I am happy to be there. At first, it was weird because I hadn't been around girls for so long, and now that's all I work with. There are about five or six girls and me. I only work part-time, though, which is good for when I start school.

I failed my driving test. I got a 70 and needed a 75. I was very upset. I made one big mistake, and he had to fail me. I rescheduled it for the following week, and with my luck, it snowed badly that week. I got canceled and rescheduled for two weeks out. I passed my second time with a 90. This is good because I have been riding the bus to work. It is stressful. Especially since there is no bus from Lake Oswego to Tualatin, and these are the two places I work at. So, I must leave extra early to be on time.

I had another interview about a week ago. It was for a business that made and distributed home goods. Apparently, it was a large company and a very reliable job.

Out of ten people, it came down to two of us. Then I was given the job. I filled out the paperwork, and one question was, "Have you ever been convicted of a felony?" Yeah, so that ruined my chance with that business. I was so close to having that job.

GETTING A SECOND CHANCE

This young man found a company that gave him a second chance. He has advanced with the company and recently was awarded a master's degree in business administration from Portland State University.

Finding an apartment with a felony is almost impossible. Some of the young men could move into their girlfriend's apartment, but if the rental agency found out that two people were living in the unit, the man had to leave since he wasn't on the lease. The young man knew he wouldn't be allowed on the lease after completing a background check. Their parole officer often sends the formerly incarcerated men to rentals in an area where there is visible drug use and fights at all hours of the night.

In addition to housing problems, relationship issues often follow the released young men. Being invited to a young man's wedding is a happy occasion. Often, the marriage doesn't last, and the man returns to square one, trying to find a place to live and deal with the emotions and stress of a breakup. It isn't easy to know how to have a successful relationship when it has never been modeled for you during your growing-up years. If children are involved, one's patience is often tested; however, the young men have learned the importance of patience and how to practice it by working with dogs. One of the sweetest videos I recently received was a former youth showing his young son how to train a dog they had recently added to their family.

Sometimes, the formerly incarcerated men need to hear words of support while showing their positive contribution to society.

OSKAR'S STORY

Oskar was born in Europe. His family consisted of four brothers, three sisters, and his mom and dad. The family kept German shepherd guard dogs that Oskar loved playing with as a child. However, a neighbor did not like the dogs' barking, so he poisoned them. Oskar's mother saved one of the dogs by pouring wine down the dog's throat.

In 1996, at age seven, Oskar and his family moved to the United States. Relatives had encouraged the family to come to the United States to start a new life. Everything was new to Oskar, and learning English was a big hurdle for him. It was not long before he got in fights at school due to students calling him racial slurs and taunting him. He did not know what was being said when called into the school office. "I was scared," he said. He was suspended from school and then faced his father with the news. His dad spanked him in hopes that would discourage future problems.

By the time Oskar was a freshman in high school, he had had enough and became a high school dropout. At age sixteen, he could get construction work and stay with friends. Before long, he was using drugs—a lot of meth and marijuana. A year later, he visited girls at a home near Portland with a friend. The girls' friends showed up sometime during the evening, and a fight broke out before long. Several of the boys were cut, and

Oskar was taken to the county jail. He was soon released and recalled, "I went back to the druggie friends and using. I rebelled against my family and didn't see my dad as a good role model. I saw parents of kids in the US giving their children attention, but not mine. My dad told me, 'Where you sleep is where you eat.'"

Two years later, one of the boys who had been beaten up filed charges against Oskar. He was charged with assault levels 2 and 3. He had a choice: fight or plea. He chose a plea and took the offer of thirty-six months. He knew his time had run out. He was now going to Oregon's most secure correctional facility for male juveniles. Oskar soon found that finishing high school was a requirement. He was nineteen and a half and only had one high school credit. For electives, he signed up for woodworking and welding. He took to woodworking and made a beautiful table that his parents now own. He was also required to participate in drug and alcohol treatment. "I soon learned that I could not go back to drugs," he said. He apologized to his parents, and they visited him weekly. On one of the visits, his dad told Oskar that he had been demoted as a counselor because he was told that if you can't keep your children out of trouble, you can't help other people keep theirs out of trouble. Oskar could now see how his actions had also hurt his dad.

At the end of each day, Oskar returned to his living unit and heard a young man talk about how much he liked working with the dogs in Project POOCH. Oskar realized he missed the dogs his family had in Europe, and being around dogs gave him joy. Oskar applied to join Project POOCH and was accepted into the program.

He was told not to go near Kiera on his first day because she only liked certain people. Oskar went to the far end of the dog yard and sat on a picnic table to observe what was going on in the program. One of the young men let Kiera out of her kennel run to see if Oskar would listen to one of his peers giving him directions. Oskar sat there, and Kiera came running over and sat beside him as if saying, "Welcome. My name is Kiera, and I'm a nice dog." The young man who let Kiera out of her kennel run couldn't believe Kiera decided immediately that she liked Oskar. After learning about animal safety, such as how to avoid dog bites, break up a dogfight, and control your dog around strangers when out for a dog walk, Oskar was allowed to work with Kiera and take her on walks around campus.

Oskar found that he was thriving, although he was locked up. He was getting treatment, school credit, job skills, and a dog that gave him a lot of attention. He was soon asked to mentor other young men with problems at the correctional facility. He was taking positive steps to become the person he and his parents would be proud of. He was getting closer to his release date and very happy. He worried about leaving Kiera behind, but we agreed that I would bring Kiera to a mutual meeting place for a visit if he stayed out of trouble.

Oskar's happiness soon turned to a big disappointment when he was informed that he had to be a US citizen before he could be released, and he had no green card. He said, "I couldn't believe it. They can't find my green card, and I am going to be deported." When one of his friends in his living unit heard about it, he told his mom, and she became an activist with no legal background, let alone any knowledge about immigration law. The other boy's mom soon got the governor involved. The big question was, how could MacLaren lose his green card? After a couple of months, the card was found in the desk drawer of a correctional worker. Oskar was happy again and just wanted to start a new life.

Project POOCH was able to pay for his first-term tuition at a two-year college as well as books for his classes through a scholarship fund funded by a donor. He also got a part-time job on campus to help pay for gas and a few extras. He went to a thrift store for clothes and spent money on little else. Along with one of the volunteers, I met him on the college campus a few times so that he could walk with Kiera and spend time with her. He was living at home with his parents again and wanted to know if Kiera could stay all night. I said, "I have to talk with your parents before I can agree to let Kiera stay overnight."

His parents approved, and we set up a crate in the garage so young children couldn't get access. I came the next day and took Kiera back to the kennel with a promise to visit again.

Oskar was good at fixing up old cars and motorcycles he purchased at auction. He would repair them and then sell them to make money to help with other school expenses. Returning to his parents' home meant attending church every Sunday and participating in and sometimes leading summer camps. He felt good being off drugs and doing the right things to move forward with his life.

One Sunday, he discovered a girl he had known when they were children, attending the same church. Oskar did not know then that she had a crush on him. She still had that crush, and Oskar became motivated to attend church regularly. They went to Bible school and prepared and taught lessons to the children. She accepted Oskar and his past. During their relationship, she took an item belonging to him, and he became upset with her. Oskar decided to write her a letter outlining why he was upset, and the situation was handled positively. Since Oskar was going to college, he wanted to be with someone with similar aspirations. "She is sweet and is not high maintenance," said Oskar.

Oskar received a lot of support and guidance from his brothers, who own a tree service and do construction work. Oskar works with his brothers and earns a decent living wage. He invited me and a few POOCH volunteers to his wedding.

He recently texted me: "You are a very good example on this earth, and I want my kids to know who you are and what you did and do for me and other people and animals. I would like you to join me and my family for lunch." When we met for lunch, Oskar insisted on paying for it, which I felt was a big enough bill with his family's meals added on. I thanked him and then sent money for him to let his children choose a toy when they went to Disneyland the following week. He sent me a video of his children with their new toys. During lunch, I observed Oskar when his young son, who was playing with a plate, sent it crashing onto the floor. Oskar quietly went to the end of the table where his son was seated and helped the server pick up the broken plate. The patrons were watching to see what would happen but saw a patient parent, not an angry parent. I was happy to observe the positive parenting skills right before my eyes.

JAKE'S STORY

Jake was another young man sentenced under Measure 11. He was seventeen at the time of his crime, a robbery in which no one was hurt, and was sentenced to five years. He and a codefendant, armed with a fake gun, robbed a home in the small town where they lived.

Jake had been in trouble before, but nothing serious. He dropped out of school because he felt no support from his teachers or parents. "I just felt no one cared," he said. He lived with his father. His mother, a felon, and his sister were in his life, but he did not live with them. There was not much going on in the small town where he lived. Alcohol and marijuana offered him what he was looking for—some good times, an escape, and some excitement. While he regretted losing his freedom and being sentenced to five years away from the life he'd known, he acclimated to MacLaren quickly, and said, "A lot was going on. I had to go to school, for one thing. There's counseling and stuff like that. There were a lot of opportunities to learn skills like the building trades."

But right from the beginning, Jake was drawn to POOCH. He remembered, "I knew about it almost as soon as I got there. Everybody does. You see all the dogs walking around campus every day. Everybody wanted to get into the program. There is a long list, and the wait can be long because only so many guys can be in it. I was there a year and a half before I got in."

Jake's favorite dog was Gabby, a cattle dog mix who had been adopted once, but her adopted family returned her. Jake described her as "aggressive toward people and toward her food, but I worked with her slowly and she fell in love with me, and she totally changed. She'd do anything I asked. We looked forward to seeing each other every day. She'd wag her tail and I'd break out in a big grin whenever I went to the kennel to take care of her. But when she was adopted, as much as I loved her, I was happy for her. And this time, the family didn't bring her back."

Through POOCH, Jake also had an opportunity to experience being a star: "A Japanese film crew came to do a documentary, and I was one of the guys they followed. At first, I thought that was really cool. I was honored to be picked, but then it got pretty hectic, and it was hard having somebody following me around all day and being hooked up to a microphone. Still, I'm proud of it."

Jake didn't like to get close to people before he went to MacLaren, but Project POOCH helped change that. He said, "I didn't care much about anybody else. I spent a lot of time alone, and that was fine with me. But at POOCH, I saw a different side of myself. I saw that I could be loving and caring. It totally changed who I was. The dogs were a huge part of that, but so were all the volunteers who came in and worked with us. Plus, all of us in the program became good friends. The whole experience brought out a gentler side of myself. I went into POOCH closed down, and now I'm loving life."

Since leaving MacLaren, Jake has gotten a job. He also coparents his young daughter. He is now working as a recruiting coordinator and will soon receive his professional certification in human resources.

MAX'S STORY

Max is another young man who had a tough upbringing: "Both my parents are alcoholics. I spent a lot of time with my grandparents. I didn't want to be at home." His parents were also high school dropouts, although his mother later got her GED. Max described his homelife: "I never had friends over because I was too afraid of what might happen if either parent had been drinking too much or smoking pot. I remember driving my parents home at age ten because they were too incapacitated to drive. I never told any of my friends about my personal life and what went on at home."

Max started doing poorly in school because too much was happening at home. He got into fistfights in elementary school and was kicked out of middle school. His dad thought the fights were self-defense. His dad had not worked in years and had plenty of time to visit the school, but he never did. Max recalled, "I started getting into serious trouble with the law and was locked up under Measure 11. I was eighteen. During the time I was locked up, my parents came to see me a total of two times. They left Oregon for a new life."

Max applied to be part of the POOCH program, remembering, "It was a little intimidating to walk into an interview and see the other young men sitting around a long table with pencils and papers ready to fire away their questions. I didn't have any experience interviewing, so I just decided to answer the best I could."

When Max was released from corrections, he started taking classes at a nearby community college. I met Max at the college library to work on a PowerPoint presentation, and he told me he was worried about the one supportive adult in his family, his grandma. "Let's go visit her," I said. When Max visited his grandma, the doctor told him that the hospital staff did not know how to improve her health. After the visit, Max wanted to tell his grandpa to get to the hospital. A short while later, his grandma passed away.

Max began having trouble concentrating on his studies, so he dropped out of college. He knew he needed to move on, but how? "I had learned to weld while locked up so I decided to see if I could find employment as a welder," Max said. "I soon found out that regardless of my skills, many employers do not want to take the risk of hiring a felon. I wasn't going to give up because I never gave up on my dogs. Always have hope. Ms. Dalton often told us about the importance of having hope."

It was not long before Max decided to try for a job in welding again: "'Yes,' I said as I pumped my arm—I got a job! I stayed focused and worked at being the best welder for the company and soon found myself getting lots of overtime hours. After several years, the economy turned bad in Oregon, and I got laid off."

Max called me, and I suggested he use his time to return to school. The yoga teacher, Roxanne, could help through a scholarship she funded. He noted, "I needed help with my math so now I'm back in school, and it feels good to be learning something I really needed. Looking back, POOCH taught me to be patient and confident that I can do good things now and in my future."

Max now has his commercial driver's license (CDL) and has been working a well-paying job as a commercial truck driver for several years.

Like those chronicled in this chapter, many of the young men in Project POOCH stay in touch and continue to let me know how they are doing. As one said recently, "I have just been through some hard times, but I knew I could make it by being patient and making ethical decisions."

26

Thoughts from Youth

JB AND ROCKY

Hands down, my favorite dog was Rocky. He was a red nose pit. I found him when I was ten; he was around one then.

One day, as I was walking back from 7-Eleven, enjoying the taste of chimichanga, I took a shortcut down North 82nd, and some thugs with bats approached me. I was stuck in a moment of shock. I didn't know whether to run or fight.

One of them cursed profanity and got close to my face. Unaware of my surroundings, this weird looking dog next to me suddenly started to growl. He was growling at the miscreants who were trying to pick a fight with me. I had never seen people run so fast.

I petted the dog and started walking home. I turned and saw that the strange dog was following me, so I took him home.

I explained to my family what had happened and how the dog had saved me from getting jumped. I asked to keep him, and they agreed. I named him Rocky. He was the most loyal companion I had for a dog. Rocky was super intelligent, too. He knew his stuff. The best part was that no one claimed him as their dog.

Rocky left us when I was sixteen. He was killed in an "accident." Some crazy driver who was not paying attention ran him over when he was crossing the road. Rocky was the best and no dog can ever be in comparison to him.

JA AND STAFF

I am writing this letter because I realized I never said goodbye before being transferred to prison. My time at Project POOCH has made me the hardworking person that I am today.

Project POOCH has changed my life in a variety of ways. One of the valuable skills I have learned was the priceless life skills taught by the staff. Sampson and Makai modeled to me every day what it means to be a man. Growing up without a father—Sampson and Makai filled that void missing in my life.

Working with dogs taught me the true meaning of compassion and respect for all forms of life. I know, without a doubt, that I wouldn't be the empathetic person I am today without Ms. D. She is the most philanthropic person I have ever met. She is the person who gave the lucky few the chance to prove that we can be rehabilitated. Ms. D. gives us positive affirmations when deserved and reprimands when needed. I will never forget our fireside chats with lectures and stories that prepared me for the world and taught me how to become a productive member of society.

Project POOCH has helped me build up my self-image and gave me a purpose in life—two things that are hard to come by in prison.

Thank you isn't enough, but I want all of you to know how appreciative I am for everything you have done for me. I hope that Project POOCH continues to thrive and that more youth at MacLaren realize the wonderful opportunity available to them. Thank you again for the experience of a lifetime.

MN AND LIFE LESSONS

Life is often a mystery at any given moment. Typically, you don't realize the lessons you learn and the impact of those learned lessons until years down the road and through life events.

As unfortunate as my circumstances may have seemed in my teenage years, I was blessed to have the opportunity to participate in the Project POOCH program.

I was separated from my mother and brother at seven as a young boy. Between the ages of seven and fourteen, I lived in multiple foster homes and group homes. During that time, there were a few bright spots. The minority of my experience was that of loneliness and uncertainty. Between the ages of fourteen and sixteen, I was homeless. By my seventeenth birthday, I was at MacLaren Youth Correctional Facility, sentenced to five years and ten months for second-degree robbery.

It wasn't until I had the chance to work with my first rescued dog through the program that I could understand what my world looked like from an outside view. In this understanding, I found inside of myself the ability to make choices, exercise patience, and put in the work that would greatly increase the outcome for this particular dog, Frank.

In a small makeshift kennel constructed of a span of chain link fencing secured to the wall on either side of the far-left corner of what seemed to me to be an old utility room that was repurposed to serve as the first Project POOCH facility sat a medium-sized black and gray cattle dog named Frank. His eyes were wide with anxiety and a posture communicated his fear and uncertainty as we watched each other, both of us somehow understanding one another. We were both safe inside our cages and, for the moment, happy we could have a somewhat predictable moment, and at the same time, we were happy that our path led to this place we shared inside this space and time. Of us, somehow understanding one another. Frank was on the cusp of euthanasia due to his inability to not bite when finding himself stressed or anxious.

I found myself experiencing my kind of social euthanasia. There we were, two young guys who had so much to give, yet our paths brought us to what seemed like, at the time, to our end.

I asked Ms. D. if it would be okay to try working with Frank one more time before he headed back to the pound. Although reluctant in the beginning, she ultimately agreed. Frank and I started our long uphill climb the next day.

During the first days and weeks, Frank and I spent much time-sharing space inside his makeshift kennel. I didn't ask much of him, and he had no expectations of me. We would sit and watch each other and occasionally share physical interaction over treats at his request. Slowly, the two of us learned to trust one another; at this point, we worked on just taking walks together with a little training sprinkled in here and there. Over the months, we had the amazing opportunity to witness change in each other for the better.

Frank eventually found a home with a young, energetic couple with another Cattle dog. Seeing Frank go was the first time I ever experienced multiple genuine emotions at once; it was new, exciting, and challenging at the same time.

Today, I can trace many life lessons I learned with Frank in that year to the lessons I have taught my soldiers in the Army, my employees, and my kids today. The biggest lesson is, "We win together, or we lose together." It is okay to depend on the people around you and do your best to draw the best out of them. I once heard a saying that ties all these things together. "If you want to run fast, run alone. If you want to run far, run together."

Frank and I never had a team; we were just two young guys doing our best to survive in an unkind world, running too fast with no real destination. Thank God for that unfriendly time and place where we found each other. I can say with certainty that our lives turned out so much better because we found each other at that particular time and place.

27

Letters from Adopted Dogs and Their Pet Parents

LETTER FROM AN ADOPTED DOG

Dear Friends,

I can hardly believe I have been in my new home for almost a week—so many new experiences in such a short time.

To start with, Friday was very busy. I had a great ride to my new home. You probably noticed that my new parents have the perfect vehicle for me—lots of room to stretch out in the back. We made a couple of stops on the way home. First, I went to Petco, where I was invited to help pick out my new bed, my set of dishes (one set for home and one set for the store I'll be at during the day with Mom and Dad), a new ball, a new Frisbee, and a new leash. The next stop was the bookstore for a book they wanted on the care of "special" dogs like me, a stop at the grocery store, and finally, home. Mom and Dad are really happy with my car manners.

I'm really happy to tell you that there is plenty of room for me and a great yard to play in.

Shortly after I arrived home, we had company, and I met a new friend named Katie—she looked a lot like me but much smaller. She's just six months old, but we played and had a great time. Bedtime was a little strange, but my new bed was good, and I slept until 6:00 a.m. Saturday.

Saturday was really an adventure. We went to our store for a couple of hours. I wore my great scarf and felt very handsome. The customers really liked me. We left around noon and went to a mall (I slept) and then to the park for a walk. I saw ducks and geese. It was really fun. Mom and Dad went to lunch after the park (I slept) and then to Grandma and Grandpa's house. Grandpa really liked petting me. They gave me a tour of their house and gave me treats. We went home for dinner and went for another walk after dinner.

By Sunday, I felt more comfortable and slept until 8:00 a.m.—Mom and Dad seemed pleased. We went for a long walk after breakfast (I think they like to take walks, and I get to go, too.) Dad played ball with me when we got home. He can really throw the ball far and high! I then met another grandma and grandpa—they had a big yard to run in and really liked me. We stopped on the way home at Costco. You should see the big bag of bones we came home with for me.

This week has been fun. I go to the store every day with Mom and Dad. They have some great customers who love dogs and come to the back room to pet me. We go for short walks during the day and longer walks after dinner. It's sometimes hard to stay in the back room when I see everything going on out front, but Mom and Dad say I have to stay there, so I really try to mind.

As you can see, I've had a busy and fun few days. Dad says when the weather is better, we'll go to the park to play Frisbee, go on hikes, go to the beach, and maybe even go camping. I really like my new home.

I think about all my old friends and miss all of you. You gave me a great beginning in life. Thank you for taking such good care of me and teaching me good manners.

LETTER FROM AN ADOPTER

Thank you for letting your puppy visit us this weekend. He is a true gentleman and a pup anyone would be proud to own. He may not have done everything perfectly while with us, but he always tried his best. He touched the nose of one of our cats and chased another, but he came right back when we called. In time, the cats (we have 5) and he would work everything out and become friends. He also met our goats. Again, he was a gentleman and waited quietly for them to sniff him. He waited to go outside like you said and never had an accident.

Unfortunately, Yankee, our dog, was not up to his old self this weekend. Yankee was really feeling his age. Both dogs seemed to like each other but didn't run and play too much because Yankee felt very old. We will take Yankee to the vet soon to see if we can change his medication and make him feel better. My only concern is that we have waited too long to get a pup for Yankee, which would be too much for him. I got them both out for one walk in the pasture, and Bear had a good time. He was so good and came right when I called him.

I know you will keep him a bit longer and finish his training. He was very good at staying and sitting, but he was not too good at down. We would like to have him over again when you think he is ready. By then, Yankee should be feeling better. Both Bear and his trainer are special people. We look forward to seeing Bear soon. I know you will keep him a bit longer and finish his training.

HAPPY DOGS AND HAPPY ADOPTERS

Hi, Everyone at Project POOCH!

I want to say THANK YOU so much for permitting me the opportunity to come into your facility and meet every one of you and your K9s! I am grateful for your hospitality and appreciate the time you all took out of your busy schedules to show me around your facilities and show me Jet's familiar environment.

I can't believe it's been two weeks since we brought this handsome boy home! First off, we changed his name to Jackson, or Jack, for short. Jackson has been an awesome addition to our family! What a great dog! Those first few days, he was a little unsure of himself, wary about moving around his new surroundings, his new kennel, our home, and our yard. I loved that he wasn't scared, just a bit unsure, and after a while, curiosity took over, and he was everywhere—upstairs, downstairs, bedrooms, kitchen, outside, etc. I love his independence as well as his acceptance of our homelife!

Jackson is now a permanent fixture beside me wherever I go and loves being where we are. I absolutely love this guy! And so does my husband! He constantly plays with Jackson and loves taking him on his three-mile daily runs! When Jack isn't with my husband, he's with my son, going for runs, riding in the car, and visiting friends' homes!

The objective of these first two weeks was to get Jack incorporated into our household routine, learn to keep paws off counters and nose out of toilet bowls, and that it's okay to venture around the yard/house exploring as much as he wants, and that when the doorbell rings, he may bark until I come to the door. He is to sit next to me quietly and on guard until I give him the command for okay or down. Sniffing is always allowed and encouraged (how else is he going to learn new things), and riding in the car means Jackson will check out a new place with new smells and possibly new dog friends! He LOVES the car!!!

Jackson's family

WHITNEY'S LETTER

Hello, Project POOCH!

Two years ago, Whitney came into our lives from Project POOCH. I still remember it as if it was yesterday. Whitney changed our lives! She is so much joy! She loves camping, going to the beach, going for walks, and playing fetch. She is also a cuddler. She loves other dogs and people—she is our social butterfly. Thank you for bringing Whitney into our lives. She is a blessing.

Whitney's family

ADELINE'S LETTER

Dear Ms. Dalton

I wanted to tell you what a positive experience dealing with Project POOCH has been for me and my family. We are now complete with lovely Adeline in our home. POOCH did a great job with her. I wanted to tell you how very impressed I was with the trainer. Boy, what a difference two months have made for him. We met him in July or August when we came to look at your program and find a companion for our family. We met Sam first, who was mentoring Adeline's trainer. As you know, Sam is a very confident and articulate young man who presented his dog, Sunshine, very well. Still new to the program, Karl had great difficulty making eye contact and looked very uncomfortable talking to us about the dog training and program. Sam was very encouraging to Karl, but dealing with us was very much out of Karl's comfort zone.

Imagine my surprise when Karl introduced Adeline to me a couple of months later. The change was remarkable. He confidently told us about Adeline's training, answered our questions, and referred us to Adam, the kennel supervisor, if he didn't know the answer.

Karl was engaging and worked with my son, teaching him how to work with Adeline.

He was patient, and I could not help but feel a sense of pride for both of them—Karl, who has come such a long way in such a short amount of time, and my son, who has never owned a dog.

Kudos to you, Ms. Dalton, for having the foresight to see that truly rehabilitating these youth is to raise the bar of what is expected of them and teach them another way to navigate the world.

Kudos to Sam for being such a positive mentor to Karl.

Kudos to Adam, Denise (volunteer), and all those who work with the youths and the dogs. It takes a village, I am sure. And to Karl, wow, how incredible it was to experience part of his helping make Adeline a wonderful companion. Adeline, who we now call Scout, and my son are becoming best friends. I am very proud of him and want to thank him from the bottom of my heart for helping make Adeline a wonderful companion. Thank you, Ms. Dalton. You have a fan club in our family. We will spread the word about Project POOCH.

Warmest regards,
A happy family

BANDIT'S LETTER

POOCH Family,

It's me, Bandit! You know me as Badger, but my family decided to call me Bandit. I guess it has something to do with me taking their stuff and running off, but I really don't see an issue.

My mommy takes me in the car a LOT. I really don't like it much, but this lady is relentless. She does give me good treats and takes me to fun places. I finally got her trained to roll down the windows so I could stick my head out, but she strapped me into some awful contraption so I could not stick my head all the way out the window.

I went to a huge park and got to meet tons of new dogs and people. I also got to go on a long walk while my sister tried to rollerblade. It's an odd sport where she falls, and I lick her. People are weird.

My mom makes me work a LOT. I take a LOT of walks twice a day and do a lot of sitting, staying, off and leaving it. This lady is bossy. The other day, she had me so busy that I fell asleep eating my bone!

I have decided to behave better and not bite so much when excited. I'm finally feeling relaxed and eating better, too. I get to sit on my daddy's lap in his huge recliner and get so much love. I'm so happy you all found me such a good home.

Love from Bandit

SCOUT'S STORY

Scout came to Lake Grove Veterinary Hospital because he was found limping in a nearby town. Karen Rake, a veterinary technician, tried unsuccessfully to find Scout's owners and hoped Project POOCH could help. Scout was young, loving, and ready to learn obedience training, but his limp caused everyone concern. Doctors at the Veterinary Referral Center of Portland offered complimentary and discounted services to have Scout's knees repaired.

The Rake family tended to Scout until he was well enough to begin obedience training with POOCH. After surgery, months of physical therapy, and weeks of obedience training, Scout's adoption was finalized; Bradlee handed over Scout's leash to the Rake family. We received the following letter from the Rakes:

Dear Project POOCH,

Since adopting Scout, he has weaved himself magically deep inside all our family's hearts. Life now would seem off balance without him sharing in our daily lives. Our son Bobby's bond with Scout deepens and strengthens every day. The look in Scout's eyes conveys many messages. He constantly shows us how devoted he is to his new family. We feel so lucky and blessed to have him.

Thank you for all you did and for allowing us to adopt him. Our lives are forever enriched for having him share his life with us.

Sincerely, The Rake Family

Bobby Rake was eight years old at the time of Scout's adoption. This is his letter in his own words:

Dear Project POOCH: This summer, I earned $123.03 From doing a Flower Stand and caring for someone's flowers while they were away—All along telling everybody about Project POOCH and that all the money I earned will go to Project POOCH.

Thanks again for Scout.

ZEKE PASSES

Dear Joan and Project POOCH,

It is with sadness I write to you and let you know my beloved dog, Zeke, whom I adopted from you, has passed away. He was an older dog when I adopted him, but we had many good years together. He loved car rides, running on the beach, and even going to the office with me on weekends. We spent very little time apart and he was a great companion and loved by my friends and family. He was wonderful with my grandsons, other dogs, and even cats. He loved Halloween and greeted the kids at the door, just sitting there and letting them pet him. We did have one problem when a little boy wanted the "Googie," not candy. He had a best friend, Sam (a springer spaniel), and they had sleepovers; we babysat Sam when his parents were out of town and when they had parties because Sam loved margaritas! Sam came last week for a few days, the first time since Zeke was gone, and we spent a lot of time cuddled in Zeke's blanket a friend had made for him. He took it hard and searched for him everywhere.

Zeke was my first dog, not the family dog or the strays my kids brought home, but a dog I chose. He protected me from squirrels and always seemed to bark at strangers who rang my doorbell and stood in front of me. He was a great comfort, and I am really taking losing him harder than I thought I would.

In the end, his body just started shutting down, and he was unable to walk, and my vet said it was time.

I was always telling his "story" to people, and what a wonderful organization you were to save him and give him a new life. Everyone thought he was just beautiful and well. No one could understand how anyone could hurt this amazing Husky. He was a blessing.

Thank you for rescuing him and allowing me to adopt him. I have lost my best friend!

An adopter

28

What's Next?

CHANGE HAPPENS

"I will never euthanize any of your dogs just because we were unable to find a forever home"; "I will ask our veterinarian for advice if a dog has an incurable disease and no longer has a quality life"—these young men had never thought such a decision might have to be made.

When I announced I would no longer lead Project POOCH, we had three dogs, Callie, Kiera, and River, without forever homes. With the help of others, I now have a small sanctuary for these beloved dogs. Former program participants know I kept my promises, and one recently sent me a text: "As you used to tell us, never give up."

I am frequently asked if I have a favorite dog, and my response is, "all of them." However, I have a favorite incident when I visited a shelter in Yamhill County, Oregon. The shelter was very small and had maybe eight dogs the day I visited. The door to the area where the dogs were housed was like a door in a home. Once the door was opened, it rested against one of the cages. I walked down the aisle of dogs and turned around to go back and start over for a second look.

When I got to the open door, I noticed a large black Labrador retriever on his hind legs doing a dance and looking straight at me with an inviting smile. The way he advocated for himself won me over. I inquired about him, and he was seven months old, fifty-eight pounds, with droopy ears. He was picked up as a stray. There was no microchip or collar. I loved his attitude and playfulness, so I loaded him up and drove him back to the kennel. He was happy, and he made me happy.

A board member and volunteer adopted him within a couple of months. He no longer had the name "Skeeter" given to him by the shelter staff. His adopter, Tracy, named him "Fenway." He had energy, and she had energy. They walked at least two miles a day, went hiking, and visited lakes and parks all over Oregon. She provided healthy meals, and later in Fenway's life, she frequently made appointments for him at specialty veterinary clinics. They were a team—bonded and enjoying life to the fullest. Tracy said, "He made me a better person. He was amazing, dignified, brave, and kind all the way to the end of his time here on Earth."

Existence has many obstacles we all face throughout our lives. The important thing is how we tackle them and move forward to fulfilling our passion, while being able to thank others for joining us and making a difference in the lives of humans and animals.

The time came to hand the reins to someone else and let go. It wasn't easy. I had already begun mentoring some of the young men as they were released from corrections. Supporting the formerly incarcerated is probably the weakest link as they step back into society. Where to live? A job? Mode of transportation? How to get a driver's license? What has changed during the time a boy turned into a young man? As a high school teacher, I guided students through their résumés and job interview experience; however, all that changed during the time they had been locked up for close to a decade or more.

MENTORING YOUTH ON THE OUTS

When Len needed transportation to a job interview, I took him to the business. When we arrived at the business where Len would apply for a job, he was told he needed to apply online. "How do I do that?" he asked. He had used a computer while in Project POOCH, but we were not connected to the Internet due to security concerns.

Another young man lacked appropriate clothing for an interview. After securing a grant from the Coleman Foundation, I instructed the young man to meet me at a clothing store for men at a mall that had been built when he was locked up. He got lost because he now had to learn how to navigate an area that he once had no problem traversing.

For those desiring to enroll in community college, I met them to pay for their tuition and books since I had the Project POOCH credit card. Our scholarship account had been well funded since several volunteers made contributions. Inner-city colleges didn't provide a place to live. Fortunately, some knew about a MacLaren volunteer who owned an apartment building, which helped a few recently released young men.

Others had to budget their time, so they studied rather than hang out with friends. Once they got their study time under control, they didn't have to use a computer in the library. The POOCH program provided a laptop, which they appreciated. Navigating their new life meant decisions were not going to be made by a corrections officer; it was now their opportunity to make their own decisions. They were no longer relegated to a certain place so they could be supervised; it was okay to walk through the many campus buildings and discover some studying in a lounge area, the cafeteria, the library, and the field area where sports were played. Observing them as they began to make a new life away from crime was exhilarating for me.

One young man confided in me that he struggled in a statistics class and didn't want to fail. I admitted that statistics was a class I had difficulty with, but talking to the professor and finding a tutor could remove his anxiety about the class.

Sometimes, I was disappointed when young men found themselves fathers and had to drop out of school and find a job to support a family. They were learning that their choices determine their future and new unthought-of responsibilities.

I recently received a text from a young man asking me when I find time to do my writing because he's trying to juggle a job and online college classes while living with his two toddlers. I responded, "Sometimes when I can't write at home, I go to the library, where it's quiet."

If a person comes from a situation where there was little role modeling on how to navigate life's obstacles successfully, I might offer suggestions after first guiding them through the steps to make their own best decisions. It is always hoped that their decision is theirs, not mine. Sometimes, I send a book they might find helpful as they travel to a brighter future.

One day, I went to a printer and had business cards made. The cards had the young man's name and the following title: Accountant in Progress. It brings me joy to let them know I'm still cheering them on and respecting their ability to make the right choices as they find and follow their passion.

Afterword

We started with one boy and one dog in 1993. When I left in 2020, we had space for thirteen dogs, and I began mentoring some young men as they began life outside the confines of a correctional facility.

Little did I know when I started Project POOCH that by pairing unwanted shelter dogs and troubled boys I would learn to forgive my father and "let it go" as I focused on respecting the young men—an integral reason why the program has succeeded in ways I never imagined. Listening to and incorporating many of their ideas empowered them and me.

One day, an adopter asked if we boarded dogs. One of the dog handlers overheard and came up with a plan: We would board the dogs of our adopters only. It became an opportunity for the young men to know that their dogs had found their forever homes and were well cared for. They tacked on a free bath the day the dog was to be picked up by the adopter. Of course, it brought more revenue to the program, and the young men completing the dog's bath always got a tip.

Too often, children are taught to silence their voices. Encouraging young people to voice their opinions or ideas is one of the steps to rehabilitation. Knowing they have added value to a project empowers the young men. By listening to them, they learned how to listen to others and their dogs.

Occasionally, a young man will contact me when he's found an abused or abandoned dog or cat in the community. He asks for resources to help a "houseless" four-legged soul. Many young men have been unhoused and know how discouraging it can be not to have a home or someone to care for them while they navigate their current situation.

WHATEVER HAPPENED TO FELIX?

Finally, after a month of back-and-forth conversations with Curtis Wagner and Garrett Fertig at the Oregon Department of Corrections, March 27, 2024, was the selected date to release Felix and let him live the rest of his life with Steven. Denise, the volunteer who went with me in 2011 to place Felix at the Oregon State Penitentiary, wanted to witness Felix's release. She and I rode together, and Steven had his own transportation.

At 6:15 a.m., Steven texted me to say he was on his way to Salem (a forty-five-minute drive from his home) and would wait for me to arrive. "Steven, we don't have to be there until 10," I replied. He let me know he was too excited to wait longer to get Felix—his pride and joy.

As usual in Oregon, it was pouring rain, so driving demanded my undivided attention. I had packed a large box full of letters, photos, and memorabilia of Felix that Steven had sent me over the years. Wagner and Fertig verified that Felix's medical records had been sent to a veterinary clinic that Steven would be using.

Denise and I arrived shortly before ten and joined Steven and Beth, the dog groomer, at the entrance. We stepped inside the visitor area and waited for Fertig and Felix to come through security. Steven chatted with staff and was proud to let them know of his recent job promotion. The room was energetic as everyone anticipated Felix's arrival. Someone yelled, "There they are!" We smiled and waited for Felix, Fertig, and two young women, Felix's caretakers.

Denise and I stood back and observed. Felix had trouble walking due to weight gain and wasn't sure what was happening. He sniffed Steven and gave him a quick lick on the face. Before long, smiles and laughter filled the area as everyone realized beloved Felix, who had been incarcerated for twelve years and three months, would be leaving.

Steven was allowed to drive his vehicle to the front entrance so Felix would not have to walk far. Steven carefully helped Felix down the many steps and into his ride home for the next chapter of his life.

Two days later, I met Steven at the First City Veterinary Clinic to learn Dr. Angela Turra's assessment. We knew Felix was overweight, but not by twenty pounds! Since Felix was fourteen years old, we anxiously awaited the physical examination results. The doctor said, "His heart sounds good." She then checked his lymph nodes and announced they were fine. Steven and I let out a sigh of relief. How much and what kind of food and exercise were discussed with Steven, noting that he would make sure Felix got everything he needed.

Dr. Turra left the room for a while, and Steven emptied the dog treat jar on the counter and filled it with water for Felix. Felix was thirsty and had no interest in special veterinary treats. We had been in the exam room for an hour, so I excused myself to go home and take care of my three dogs.

I followed up with Steven to see how things were going. He responded, "I'm taking a week off from work to be with Felix. We are doing four forty-five minute walks, and he is meeting other dogs."

Felix made a huge difference in Steven's life and did so for many other adults in custody at the penitentiary. A dog program is now being planned so that the human-animal bond can help the incarcerated experience the difference dogs can make in rehabilitation.

PRESENTING RESEARCH IN JAPAN

In 2004, I traveled to Japan to present my research about the human-animal bond with others. Veterinary Inspector at the Japan Animal Welfare Society Yamaguchi Chizuko responded to my abstract. An excerpt of her comments follows:

> It pleases me to know that the dogs themselves also gain a happy new life after leaving the institution and end up with kind owners in warm homes. However, this kind of project is only possible (and should only be allowed) under the following criteria, namely that the welfare and happiness of the animals (in terms of good mental and physical care) is guaranteed, that the environment is ideal, that the associated training is nonstressful, and that the dogs are treated with responsibility and consideration.

It took many requests to get Felix released to Steven. Felix now lives outside the walls in a community where he goes for long walks and enjoys outdoor activities with Steven. (Photo by Nancy Hill.)

Acknowledgments

I am incredibly grateful to my exceptional editor, Andrea Kathryn Gapsch, Purdue University Press. Andrea's guidance and wisdom have been remarkable in our working relationship. She always got back to me immediately when I had questions or needed advice. If she was going to be away from the office, I was given advance notice to prepare for any delays should I have questions. Her team, Justin Race, Chris Brannan, and Bryan Shaffer, have been flexible and involved me in much of the decision-making for the book's cover. Others behind the scenes, manuscript reviewers Katherine Purple, Kelley Kimm, and the Purdue Board, weighed in on the manuscript and made valuable suggestions for improvement. All of you are rock stars, thank you. Creativity and professional skills produced a well-designed and well-thought-out result of *Second Chances: The Transformative Relationship Between Incarcerated Youth and Shelter Dogs*.

When the world turned to the Internet rather than in-person learning in 2020, I discovered an online writing class led by Jack Canfield. The class provided an opportunity to get feedback on my manuscript from Jack. I listened to his words of wisdom, which led me to Mary Lou Reid, book coach at Steve Harrison's *Get Published Now*. I could not have been paired with a better coach. Thank you, Mary Lou. Deb Englander provided examples of winning proposals. I am amazed to be gifted with such competent people who have guided me through getting my story of dogs helping incarcerated youth in print.

I appreciate the research of many recognized experts in the Human-Animal Bond. Thank you, Randy Lockwood, Phil Arkow, Alan Beck, Frank Ascione, Arnold Arluke, and Lynette Hart, for your groundbreaking research. All of you have done much-needed research, which has been a tremendous help to me.

Bill Johnson, Willamette Writers, thank you for your meticulous review of my query and kind words about the subject of my book. (I know you know how sensitive writers can be about their work.) Nancy Hill, thank you for putting your writing aside to be my reader and accountability partner. You listened when I called in tears over reliving the trauma of my dad killing my dog. Nancy, you were patient and kind through the ups and downs of the writing process. You also published articles about Project POOCH and used your professional skills to photograph all our fundraising events. I shall always be grateful. Linda Hines, Executive Director of the Delta Society (now known as Pet Partners), secured $10,000 from a donor to begin building our first area to house two dogs and needed supplies.

Tracy Lucas, Mark Oronzio, and Sandy Zimmer were the first volunteers at Project POOCH. I could always count on you to be ready to do whatever needed to be done at the kennel. I value your friendship and how well you worked with the youth on various assignments. I know they appreciate all they learned from you about Photoshop, so their dog flyers would look the best. Remembering them on their birthdays and holidays always brought smiles from the youth.

Many others came forward to help with the first on-site dog program in juvenile corrections. Debra Yates published my questionnaire in a free newspaper available throughout Oregon. What Pets Teach Us brought two boxes of returned questionnaires to add to the ones I collected while living in New York. Unity World Healing Center, Reverend Victoria Etchemendy, for free meeting space and office space for our first fabulous assistant, Brie Caffey; Dr. Scott Lozier, Northwest Veterinary Specialists, for saving the fractured leg of Rufus, the abused dog, at no charge. Veterinarians of the Veterinary Referral Center of Portland, Woodburn Veterinary Clinic, Slocum Veterinary Clinic in Eugene; veterinarians at the various shelters and humane societies for complimentary vaccinations; Donors—Jean Vollum, Sophie Engelhard-Craighead, Frank and Julie Jungers, Maggie Hayes, Carol Butler, and Dave's Killer Bread for providing funding for kennels, education center, and medical fund; Stan Bland, Charlie Allis, Dee Anderson, Tom Lang, Barbara Coles, Suzanne McKim, Ellen Bye, Dave and Susie Waki, Fred Carter, CPA; Steve Seymour, attorney; Barbara King, Youth Coach; Ted, and Beverly Paul and Salem volunteers: Estelle Watson, Kathy Gardner, Donna Mitchell, Debbie West, and Turise Henthorn. Thank you for showcasing POOCH in the Salem area regularly. Thank you for your commitment and dedication. Many donors (some as young as five) made cash and in-kind donations. Thank you to every person who gave their time and resources to make the program successful. In many ways, your funding, ideas, and dedication provided much-needed support to the program and opportunities for the youth and dogs to dispense with unacceptable behavior and become shining examples of second chances for both.

The corrections staff: Adam Bergin, Tom Anhalt, Richard Beck, Joseph Start, Dustin Boos, Wynton Cox, Robert Ford, Andre Johnson, Elray Sampson, and Makai Brusa supervised the kennel, and they stressed the importance of accountability and that there were consequences for any lapses in behavior expectations. The staff were father role models for many—Dan Berger, superintendent, for your continued support of the program. Thank you, thank you. I didn't know until there was a fistfight in the school how important the security staff on campus was. They were unsung heroes. They didn't take their jobs lightly. Doug Lawson surprised the youth when he brought his pet pig for show and tell. Steve Spencer, thanks for spending time with your Belgian Malinois and the youth with search and rescue demonstrations. The maintenance crew has been exceptional from the very beginning, providing certified electricians, plumbers, and groundskeepers when needed.

Thank you to the Verizon team for guiding the youth in building the rain shelter in the yard behind the education center. You listened to the youth and incorporated some of their ideas.

After much of the writing of my manuscript, I was fortunate to have the assistance of computer experts Sara Chesney and Cheryl Hill, West Linn librarians, and librarians at the Canby and Lake Oswego libraries. Mark Webber, Nay Zuniga of Webber Consulting, Inc., and Jeffrey Martinez, thank you for your creative ideas and joyful attitude while developing my website (joandalton.com/author/second chances).

There are many others to whom I am grateful for how you helped the program from the beginning and shared your skills and ideas to make the program a model for others. Architect Jane Turville involved the youth in planning the education center and brick kennels. The Schommer & Sons Construction team allowed the youth to work alongside them. I sincerely appreciate everyone who gave time, energy, skills, and donations to the program over the years.

Laurie Christensen and Colin Ma, thank you for adopting Pete, the Border collie, when the shelter didn't consider him adoptable. Thanks to Colin, he's now a star in agility. I appreciate your friendship and energy as you continue to provide fundraising products and financial help.

Tom Steinhoff for working in the office and demonstrating temperament dog testing to participants in POOCH 101. Richard Phillips and Jessi Pierce of Stumptown Racers, Kate Stebbins-Stinson, and the Cascade Sled Dog Club for the scooters and training harnesses for the youth to learn skijoring with their dogs. Lauren McCall for teaching the youth about T-Touch training for dogs; Jill Mohr for teaching the youth positive reinforcement dog training; Devin Gorsage, Dog Behaviorist; Cinthia Mitchell, Doggone Fun Doggy Daycare, for working with the youth in the earlier years of Project POOCH and offering employment opportunities.

Michele Driscoll, your perspective and feedback were valued in the office and as a manuscript reader. Susie and Shar ran the community outreach office well and made much-needed suggestions. Later, the program was enhanced with the following support staff: Jan, Barbara, Juanita, DeVida, Eleanor, Kelsey, and Rena. Doug Brewer, thank you for being our pro bono computer troubleshooter. Bob Shelstad, thank you for supervising the first two POOCH youth over the weekends. I appreciated the breaks. Dr. Richard Werner came out of retirement to teach the youth what veterinarians look for when a dog is brought to them for evaluation. He taught the youth as if they were already veterinarians. Dr. Debbie Unrau visited the kennel every month to provide lessons about dogs and answer questions from the youth. Carol Shiveley, Education Director, Oregon Humane Society, recommended dogs for the program, gave presentations, and served on the POOCH Board. Dee Anderson, Suzanne McKim, and Barbara Coles served on the board.

What would I do about the three dogs no one wanted to adopt? I knew I couldn't live with myself if I walked away from these dogs when I left the program in late 2019. Dolores Smith, Lloyd Wood, Tracy Lucas, Mark Oronzio, Roxanne Thomas, and others funded me to bring the three dogs to the country where no one cares if dogs bark. They can run free in their fenced area and live out the last chapter of their lives. When one of the dogs, Kiera, later collapsed in the yard, Pamela Owen came to help get her to the emergency clinic for our final goodbye. Thank you, Pamela.

Bill Caffey, you cheerfully offered to drive to the southern part of the state and stay all night until the shelter opened so you could pick up an unclaimed POOCH dog, Curly. Denise Mason, the best tester of shelter dogs, provided detailed information about many dogs selected for the program. Your feedback on my manuscript was invaluable—especially on what to keep and delete. Thanks for adopting Curly and seeing him through his time on Earth.

The many others to whom I am grateful for how you helped the program from the beginning and shared your skills and ideas to make it successful. Whether you gave time, talents, donations, or advice over the years, you are part of what the program became—a way for youth and dogs to transform for a better life. You and the dog adopters showed the youth that they can make a positive difference and get on the path to success.

Perrin Damon, I enjoyed working with you as a co-leader the year before I left the program. Your background in corrections and networking brought Kristi Racer, Oregon Youth Authority Research and Evaluation, to provide current research on youth recidivism in 2018.

The Lougheed family welcomed me to live with them and their children for a year. Although my gratitude is late, your guidance shall always be remembered.

Thank you to the youths' families for visiting the kennel on family day for a relaxed visit and lunch. Whether working together for a common goal at the kennel or celebrating a birthday, the youths often said, "We're like family here." Thank you to First Mate Dog Food for donating food to dogs transferred from POOCH to my sanctuary every month.

After reading *Second Chances: The Transformative Relationship Between Incarcerated Youth and Shelter Dogs*, I hope you will consider helping youths and dogs in your local area.

Appendix 1: Terminology

CANTEEN: on campus, a place to eat or buy candy, soda, etc.
CIU: Crisis Intervention Unit
D & A: drug and alcohol
DOC: Department of Corrections
FLATS: bathroom
HIGH TAG: the highest status
ISSUES: things or problems people need to work on
JUVIE: juvenile
MHP: mental health professional
OC: off campus
OUT OF GROUP: youth sits in a chair and faces the wall (consequence for not following rules)
OUTS: outside the juvenile facility
PRIVS: privileges
RUNNERS: people who escape or attempt an escape
SO: sex offender
UPSTATE: adult prison
VO: violent offender

Appendix 2: Class Rules and Expectations for Success

PROJECT POOCH CLASS RULES

1. This class uses positive reinforcement, so please do not use choke chains or prong collars. Such collars are considered contraband.
2. We use nylon or leather collars and leashes.
3. Please allow your dog potty time before coming to class, as we may be inside buildings.
4. Your dog MUST have the following vaccinations: Distemper/Parvo combo (which may look like DHLPPC or DH2P), Bordetella, and Rabies. Please bring a copy of these vet records to the first class. A licensed veterinarian must have administered them.
5. Please bring numerous soft treats cut into approximately quarter-inch pieces. They need to be small enough for the dog to eat quickly and be ready right away for the next command.
6. Please be open-minded and ready to have a good time with your dog, creating an everlasting bonding experience you and your dog will appreciate forever.

EXPECTATIONS FOR SUCCESS

Our Mission: To learn responsibility, patience, and compassion for all life.

Expectations:

Work with the dog assigned to you.

Work with other youth.

Wear appropriate attire—uniform shirt—NO SWEATS.

Duties include:

Clean kennels and yards, walk, train, brush, comb, bathe, and check over dogs for fleas, infections, scratches, cuts, bite marks, and runny eyes. Check feces (poop) for inconsistencies, such as diarrhea, worms, foreign objects, etc.

Feed and water dogs in the amount directed. Check to see if the dog assigned to you has special food requirements.

When walking outside the kennel area, keep your dog on a leash. Keep a Project POOCH tag on your dog. Assign someone to care for your dog in your absence.

Know and keep records of your dog. Know the breed, approximate age, and weight, and be able to tell visitors about your dog and any other dogs you know about in POOCH.

Keep your personal belongings at your desk and clean up after yourself.

Keep the inside and outside of the kennel always clean. This will impress visitors who come in at any time.

Cover the food cans to avoid attracting unwanted critters to the kennels.

NO contraband is to be in the kennel or work area (girlie magazines, chew, drugs, non-dog DVDs, etc.) Follow directives given by supervisors.

NO headsets in the work area. NO commercial television unless authorized by supervisors. The TV is for training videos. Read articles the supervisors assign you to read.

Conduct yourself in a manner that is an asset to the program and yourself.

I, ________________________________, have read this and agree to follow these rules so I will be successful in Project POOCH. I also understand that disciplinary action or dismissal may result if I do not follow these rules.

Date ______________ Witness ____________________________

Appendix 3: Recommended Resources

BOOKS

Animals as Teachers and Healers by Susan Chernak McElroy

Bridging the Bond by Tami L. Harbolt

Children and Animals by Frank R. Ascione

Compassion: Our Last Great Hope Selected Speeches by Leo K. Bustad

Do Over Dogs: Give Your Dog a Second Chance for a First Class Life by Pat Miller

Feisty Fido by Patricia B. McConnell and Karen B. London

How Animals Help Students Learn by Nancy R. Gee, Aubrey H. Fine, and Peggy McCardle

On Talking Terms with Dogs by Turid Rugaas

The Culture Clash by Jean Donaldson

The Other End of the Leash by Patricia McConnell

Your Outta Control Adopted Dog by Eve Adamson

CONFERENCE PROCEEDINGS

"The Pet Connection," Proceedings of the Minnesota-California Conferences on the Human-Animal Bond, edited by Robert K. Anderson, Benjamin L. Hart, and Lynette A. Hart, 1983.

"People and Animals: A Global Perspective for the 21st Century," 9th International Conference on Human-Animal Interactions (IAHAIO), 2001.

"People and Animals: A Timeless Relationship," 10th International Association of Human-Animal Interaction Organizations (IAHAIO), 2004.

MONTHLY SUBSCRIPTIONS

Cornell Dog Watch, expert information from the Cornell Richard P. Riney Canine Health Center.

The LINK Letter, The Global Resource Center on the LINK between Animal Abuse and Human Violence, www.nationallinkcoalition.org.

Whole Dog Journal, a complete guide to natural dog care and training.

DOG TRAINING VIDEOS

Ian Dunbar, DVM, dog training and behavior, online courses, seminars, and workshops from www. DunbarAcademy.com.

Patricia B. McConnell, PhD, www.theotherendoftheleash.com.

DOG TRAINERS

Certified Professional Dog Trainers (CPDT)—highly recommend this certification vs. no certification. CPDT applicants must take written and experience tests to receive certification. They recommend reward-based dog training—no force training.

OTHER

Corrections Education Association, P.O. Box 14429. Norfolk, VA 23518.

National Link Coalition, working together to stop violence against people and animals.

Office of Juvenile Justice and Delinquency Prevention (OJJDP) is a component of the Office of Justice Programs within the United States Department of Justice. Its mission is to prevent and respond to youth delinquency and victimization.

"Reforming Juvenile Justice: A Developmental Approach," Report Brief, National Academies Press, 2012, www.nap.edu.

About the Author

Joan K. Dalton's work as a school administrator in Oregon's most strict lockup for incarcerated boys inspired her to start Project POOCH (Positive Opportunities—Obvious Change with Hounds), which involved pairing the boys with problem shelter dogs. Her work has been published in *Dog Fancy, Cat Fancy, Our Animal Wards,* and *Northwest Magazine,* and her experience with Project POOCH has been featured on Animal Planet. Currently, Dalton uses her experience as a business teacher and consultant to mentor formerly incarcerated youth. To learn more, visit Joan's website www.joandalton.com.

Rufus, the abused dog, found a home with Joan. (Photo from author's collection.)

www.ingramcontent.com/pod-product-compliance
Lightning Source LLC
Chambersburg PA
CBHW050448100425
24908CB00002B/2

9781626711051